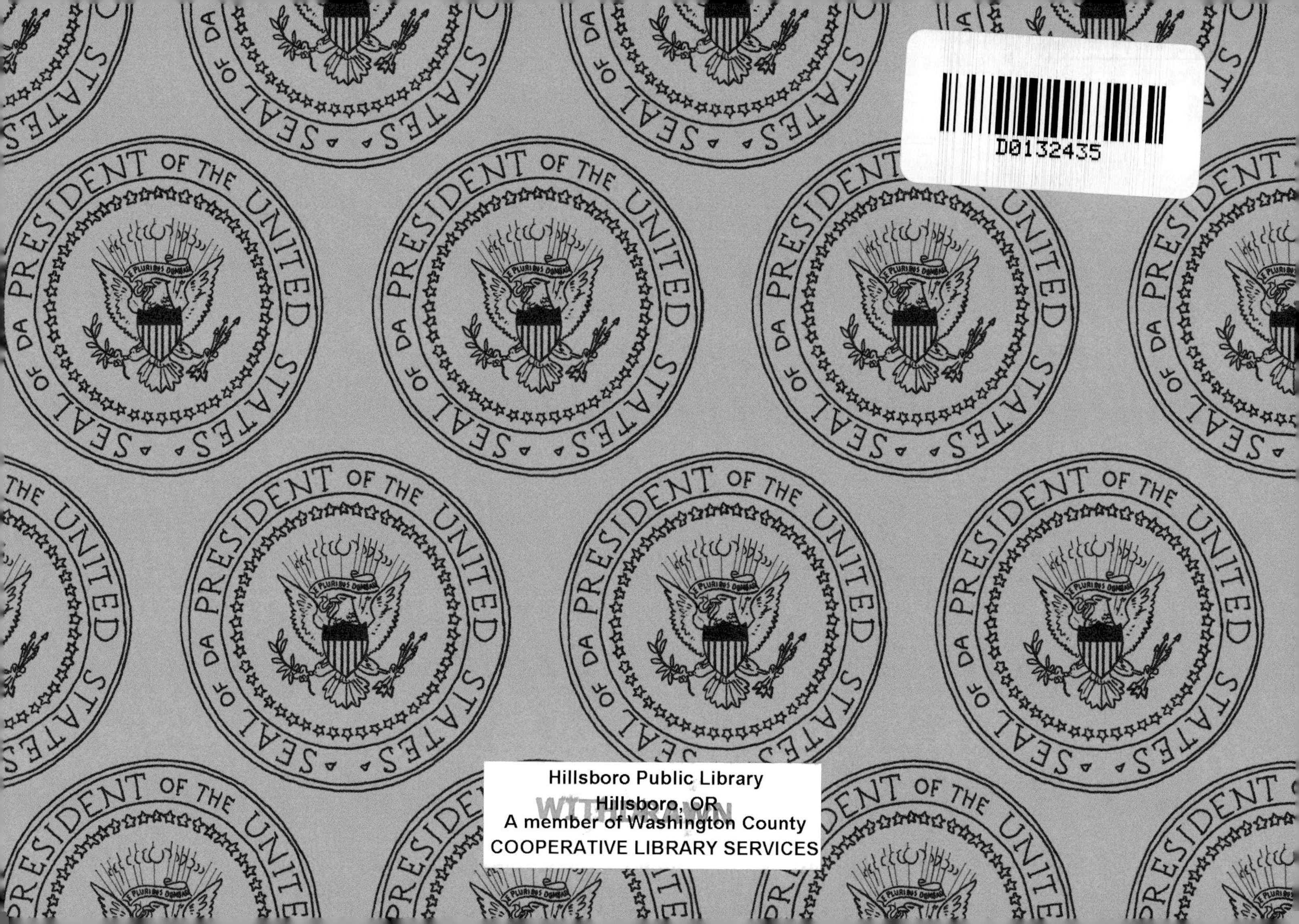
SEAL OF DA PRESIDENT OF THE UNITED STATES
E PLURIBUS DUMBASS

LIL' DONNIE

EXECUTIVE PRIVILEGE

BY MIKE NORTON

Mike Norton
@themikenorton | ihatemike.com

Copy edits by Sean McKeever
@seankmckeever | seanmckeever.com

Book design by Sean Dove
@andthankyou | andthankyouforflying.com

Lil' Donnie, Vol. 1. First printing. August 2018. Published by Image Comics, Inc. Office of publication: 2701 NW Vaughn St., Suite 780, Portland, OR 97210. Copyright © 2018 Mike Norton. All rights reserved. "Lil' Donnie," its logos, and the likenesses of all characters herein are trademarks of Mike Norton, unless otherwise noted. "Image" and the Image Comics logos are registered trademarks of Image Comics, Inc. No part of this publication may be reproduced or transmitted, in any form or by any means (except for short excerpts for journalistic or review purposes), without the express written permission of Mike Norton, or Image Comics, Inc. All names, characters, events, and locales in this publication are entirely fictional. Any resemblance to actual persons (living or dead), events, or places, without satirical intent, is coincidental. Printed in CANADA. For international rights, contact: foreignlicensing@imagecomics.com. ISBN: 978-1-5343-0977-7.

33614080722779

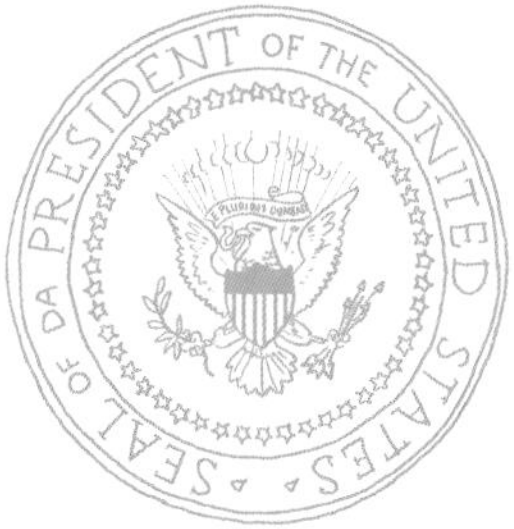
SEAL OF DA PRESIDENT OF THE UNITED STATES

INTRODUCTION

By Daniel Kibblesmith

When I was around six, I discovered the comic strip, *Doonesbury.*

Doonesbury, if you're not familiar, is the story of somewhere between two and fifteen interchangeable men with rectangular noses, who may or may not live in Washington D.C., and wear glasses (or sunglasses) and talk about Ronald Reagan. My favorite character was the talking cigarette. I think he represented cigarettes.

Doonesbury Cartoonist Gary Trudeau, if you're reading this collection of Mike Norton's LIL' DONNIE comic strips (and you should!), I apologize for nothing. I was six. You were riffing on Iran Contra next to *Broomhilda* and *Mother Goose & Grim.*

HEY, SPEAKING OF GRIM.

I'm a grownup now, so I totally "get" "politics." As a writer for *The Late Show With Stephen Colbert,* I spend most of my waking hours listening to, transcribing, and regurgitating the ramblings of the 45th and current President of The United States, Donald John Trump.

But I know I'd still be obsessing over the minutiae of this presidency regardless. I find myself taking out my phone in restaurants or long traffic lights to check if major American cities are still standing, or if one of his grown sons ate a bug. So do you, I bet.

So why do I love Mike Norton's LIL' DONNIE, so much? How could I possibly have room for more Trump in my media diet?

Firstly, the craft that goes into it. Norton is an exceptional cartoonist. His superhero art does more than tell the story for me, it gives me the feeling of clashing action figures in my hands, forever shiny and on-model. But this comic strip format is no exception. The caricatures in LIL' DONNIE are spot-on emotional likenesses, from the exhausted General Kelly, to puffy-faced walking corpse, Steve Bannon, to Vladimir Putin's smoldering eternal shirtlessness. If you're going to make any standout satire about Donald Trump at this point, you're going to have to earn people's eyeballs – and LIL' DONNIE is rendered in equal parts hideousness and beauty.

Then there's the jokes! Nothing against the world of Late Night Comedy™, but LIL' DONNIE is a comic strip, which means everything is on the table. Trump meets the ghost of MLK in this comic. The White House is besieged by Muppets. Future Barron Trump drives through a radioactive Mad Max hellscape. At one point, the president is briefly replaced by a sloth. LIL' DONNIE goes to the weirdest, saddest, funniest places in Norton's brain to make its points, and to make us feel briefly sane and comforted.

But maybe the best reason to read LIL' DONNIE – and to collect the strips in a physical book – will be to REMEMBER. These comics aren't just a series of gags, they're a chronicle of what it was like to try and keep up with a shifting reality during this era of humanity. Rereading these strips in future years will be like rewatching season one of the fall of western democracy. Remember Anthony Scaramucci? Rex Tillerson? Sean Spicer? Actually, I'm not sure Sean Spicer ever existed, but you get the point.

As far as I know, comic strips are a medium still occasionally discovered by children. Maybe those satirists of the future will discover this volume, and experience a vague inkling of the adult world, a time capsule of unfamiliar names and grownup crises hopefully long past. A new *Doonesbury* to be stumbled upon by the little Barack Khaleesi Nakamuras and the Lin-Manuel Steinbergs born in 2027 who won't know how good they have it, or won't believe how good WE had it, depending on how this all shakes out.

Good luck!

Daniel Kibblesmith
2018

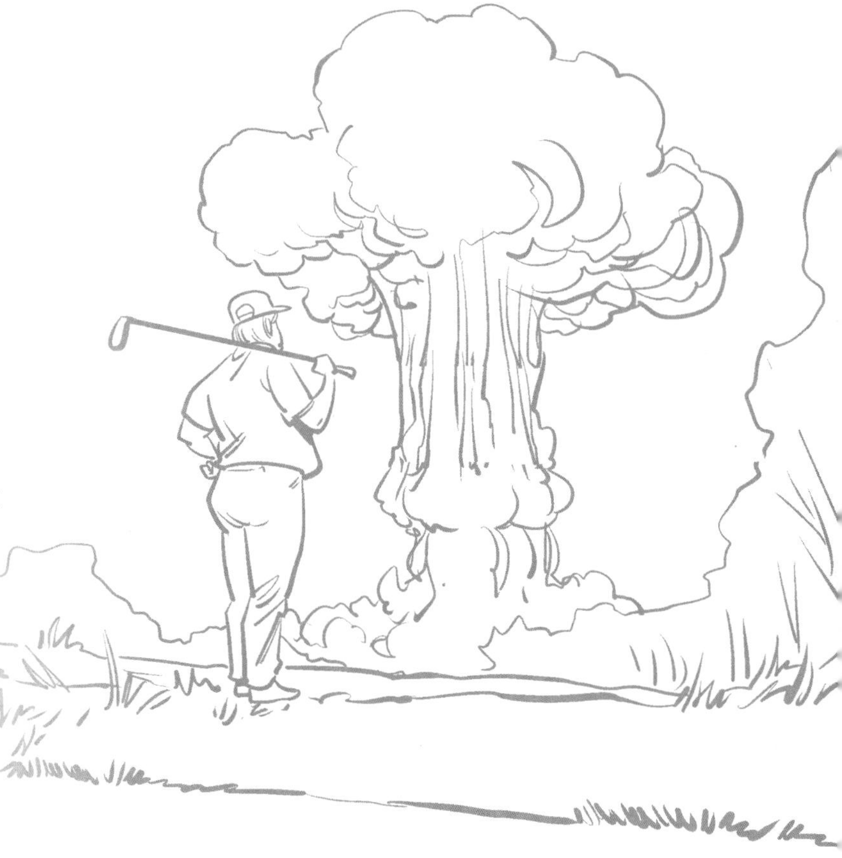

Feb 2, 2017

Lil' Donnie

by Mike Norton

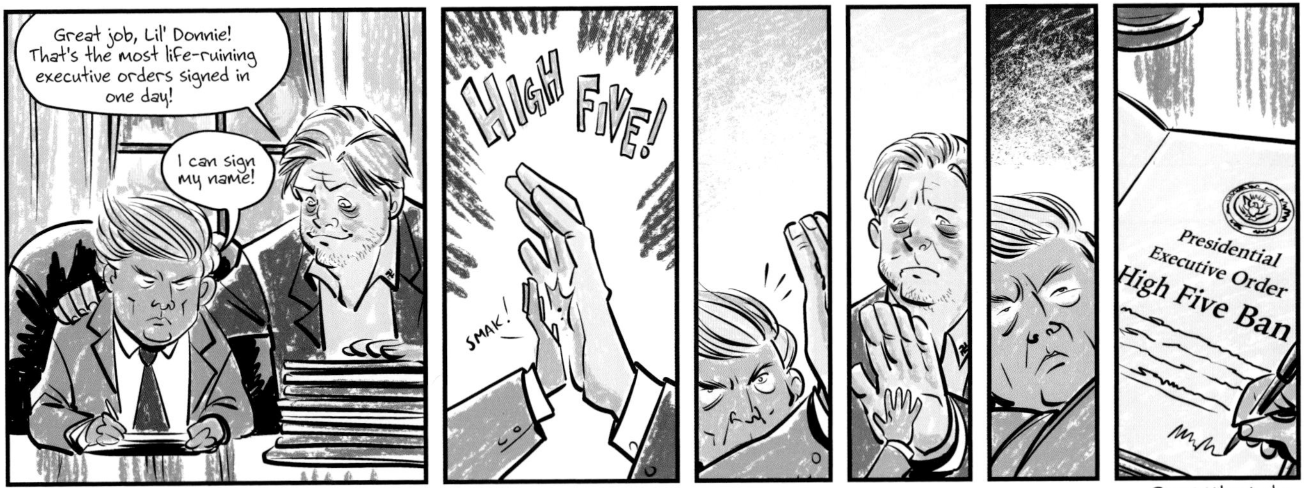
Great job, Lil' Donnie! That's the most life-ruining executive orders signed in one day!
I can sign my name!
HIGH FIVE!
SMAK!
Presidential Executive Order
High Five Ban

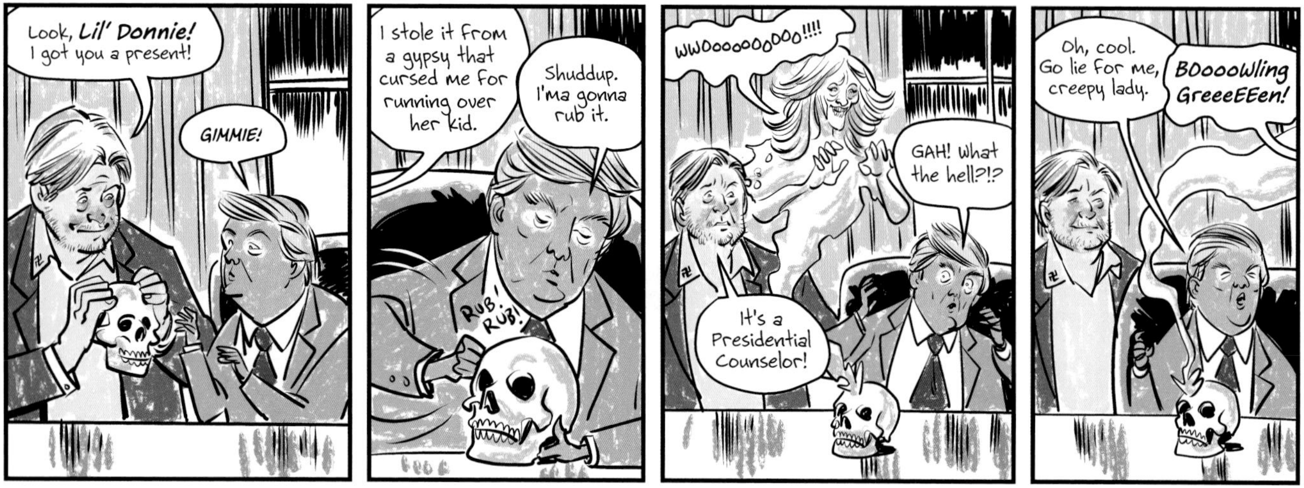

Look, *Lil' Donnie!* I got you a present!
GIMMIE!
I stole it from a gypsy that cursed me for running over her kid.
Shuddup. I'ma gonna rub it.
RUB! RUB!
WWOOOOOOOOOO!!!!
GAH! What the hell?!?
It's a Presidential Counselor!
Oh, cool. Go lie for me, creepy lady.
BOooOWling GreeeEEen!

Feb 5, 2017

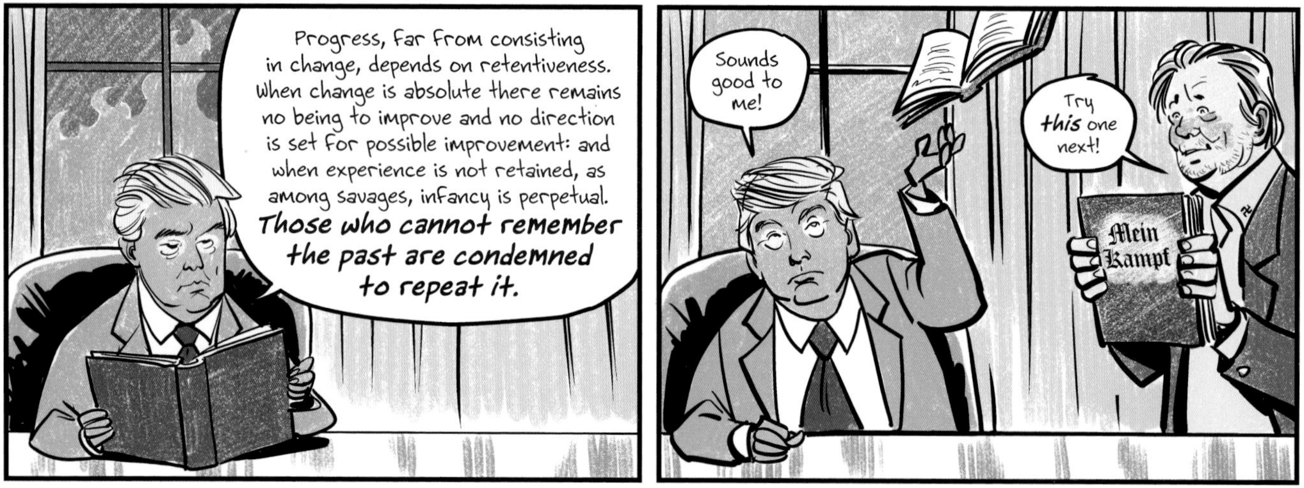

Progress, far from consisting in change, depends on retentiveness. When change is absolute there remains no being to improve and no direction is set for possible improvement: and when experience is not retained, as among savages, infancy is perpetual. **Those who cannot remember the past are condemned to repeat it.**
Sounds good to me!
Try *this* one next!
Mein Kampf

Feb 5, 2017

Feb 6, 2017

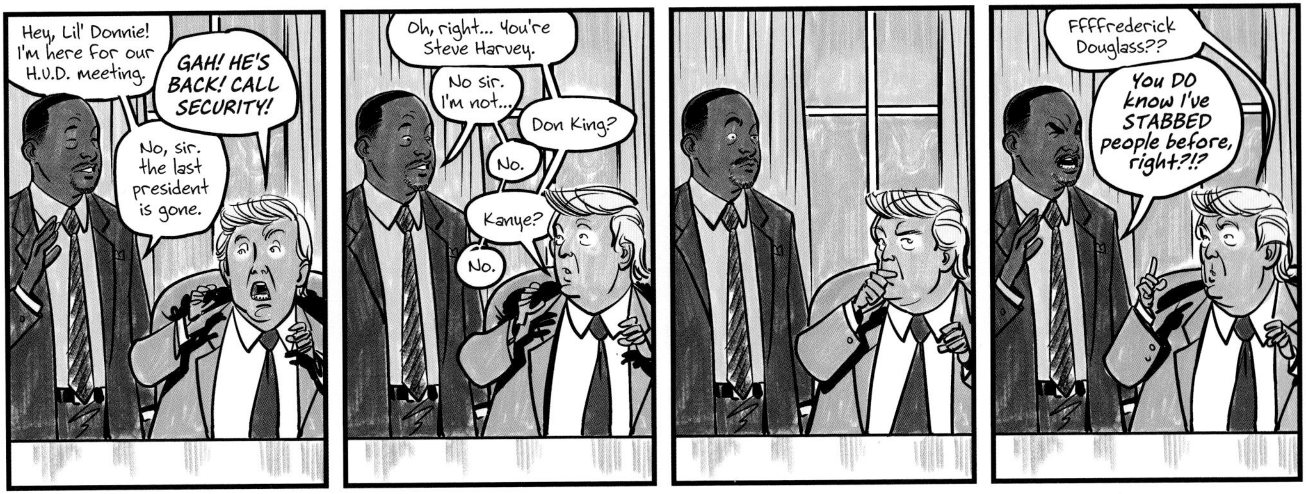
Hey, Lil' Donnie! I'm here for our H.U.D. meeting.
GAH! HE'S BACK! CALL SECURITY!
No, sir. the last president is gone.
Oh, right... You're Steve Harvey.
No sir. I'm not...
Don King?
No.
Kanye?
No.
Ffffrederick Douglass??
You DO know I've STABBED people before, right?!?

Feb 7, 2017

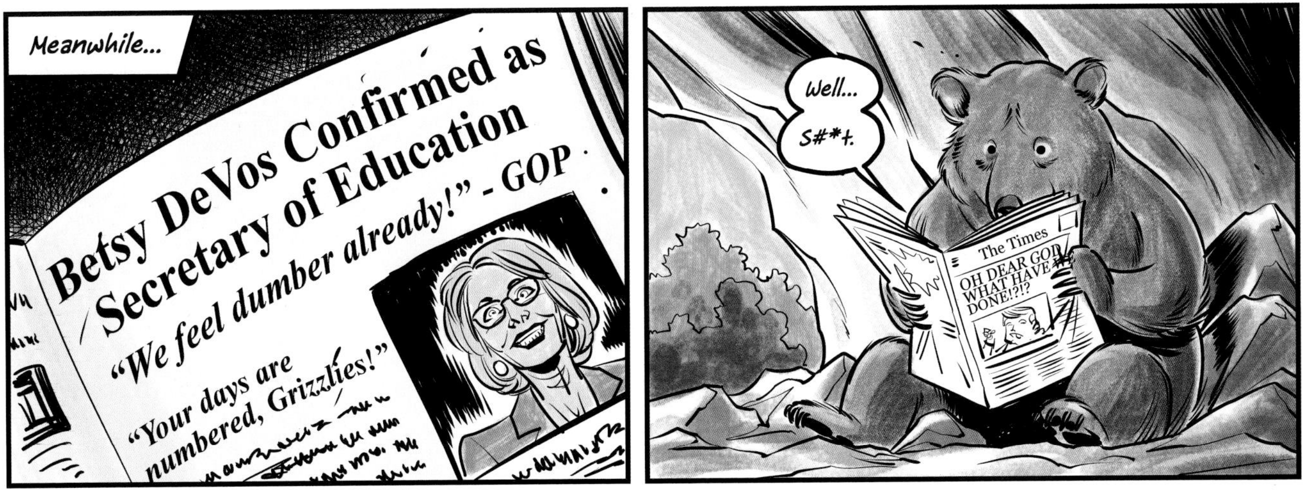
Meanwhile...
Betsy DeVos Confirmed as Secretary of Education
"We feel dumber already!" - GOP
"Your days are numbered, Grizzlies!"
Well...
S#*t.
The Times
OH DEAR GOD
WHAT HAVE
DONE!?!?

Feb 10, 2017

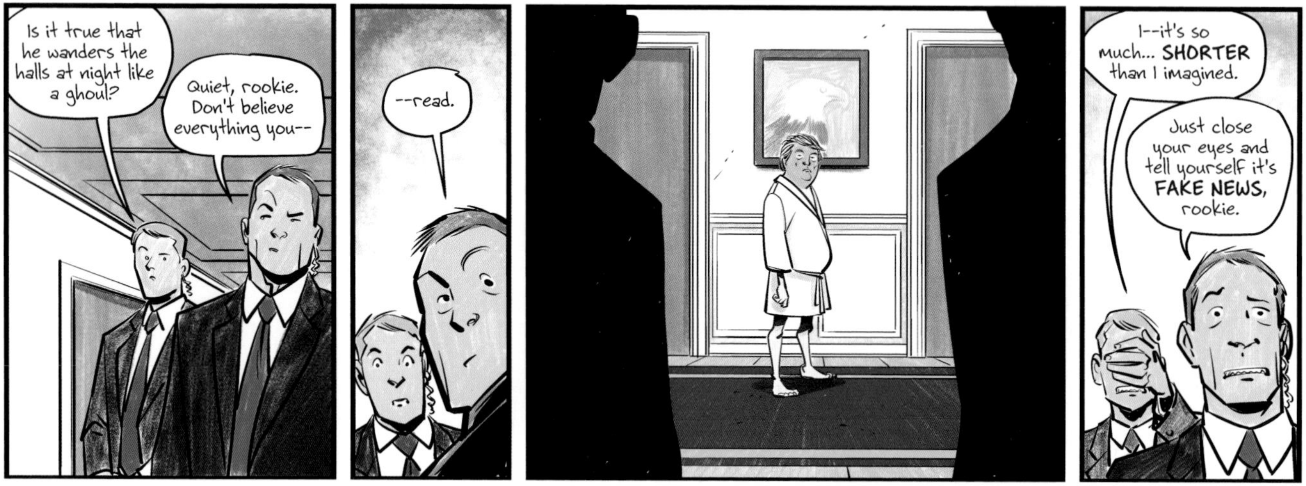
Is it true that he wanders the halls at night like a ghoul?
Quiet, rookie. Don't believe everything you--
--read.
I--it's so much... **SHORTER** than I imagined.
Just close your eyes and tell yourself it's **FAKE NEWS,** rookie.

Feb 12, 2017

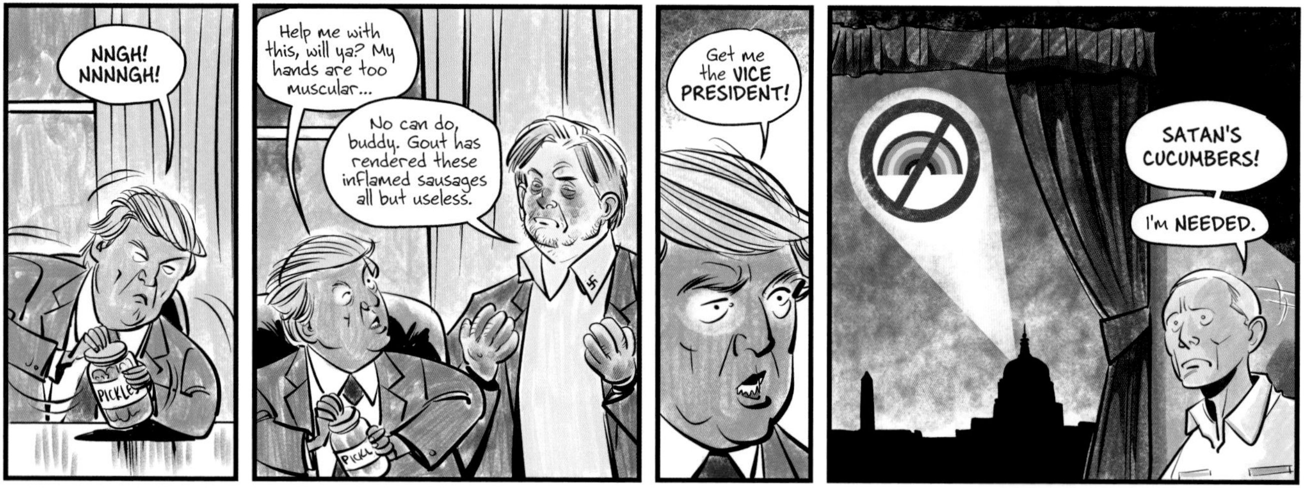
NNGH! NNNNGH!
Help me with this, will ya? My hands are too muscular...
No can do, buddy. Gout has rendered these inflamed sausages all but useless.
Get me the **VICE PRESIDENT!**
SATAN'S CUCUMBERS!
I'm **NEEDED.**

Feb 13, 2017

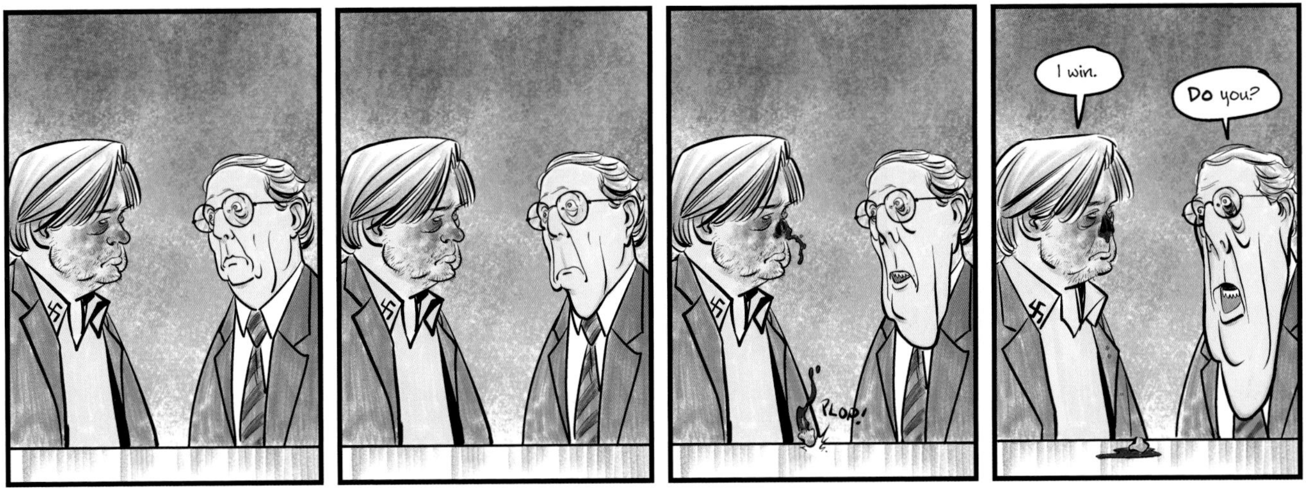
PLOP!
I win.
Do you?

Feb 23, 2017

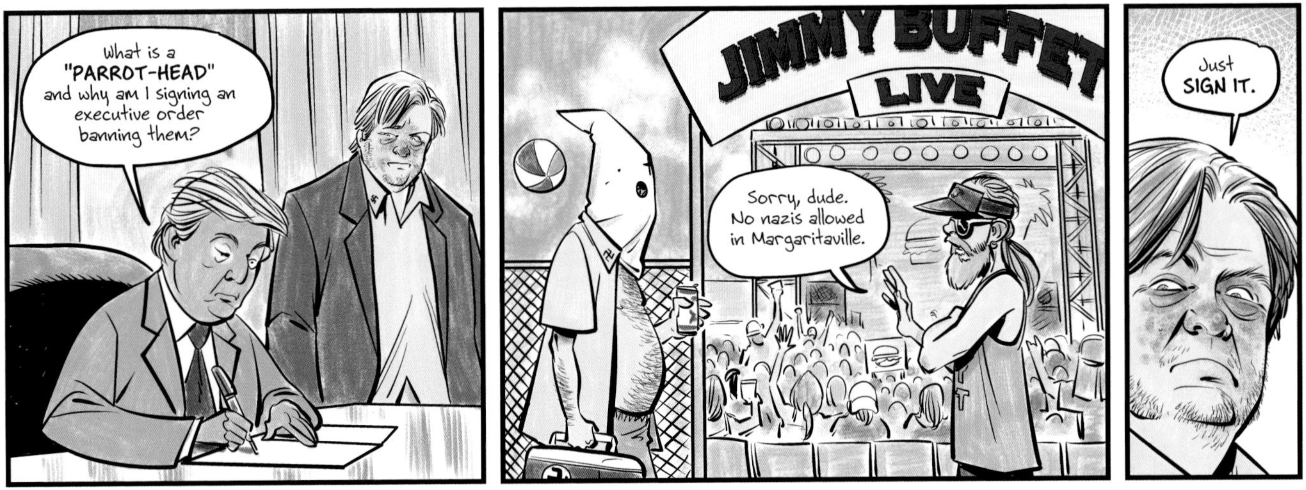
What is a "PARROT-HEAD" and why am I signing an executive order banning them?
JIMMY BUFFET
LIVE
Sorry, dude. No nazis allowed in Margaritaville.
Just SIGN IT.

Feb 14, 2017

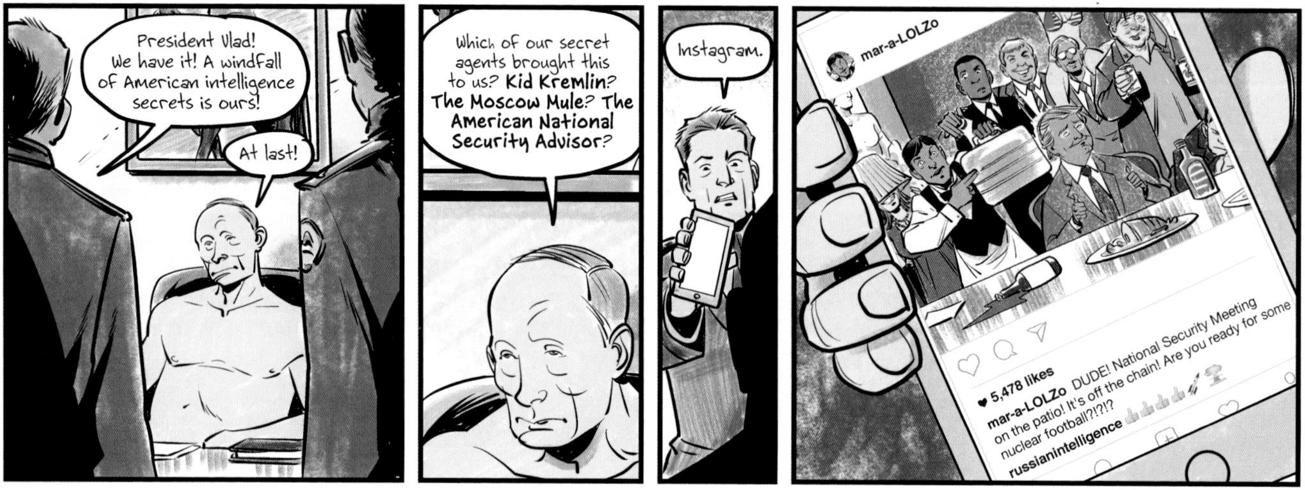

President Vlad! We have it! A windfall of American intelligence secrets is ours!
At last!
Which of our secret agents brought this to us? Kid Kremlin? The Moscow Mule? The American National Security Advisor?
Instagram.
mar-a-LOLZo
5,478 likes
mar-a-LOLZo DUDE! National Security Meeting on the patio! It's off the chain! Are you ready for some nuclear football?!?!?
russianintelligence

Feb 15, 2017

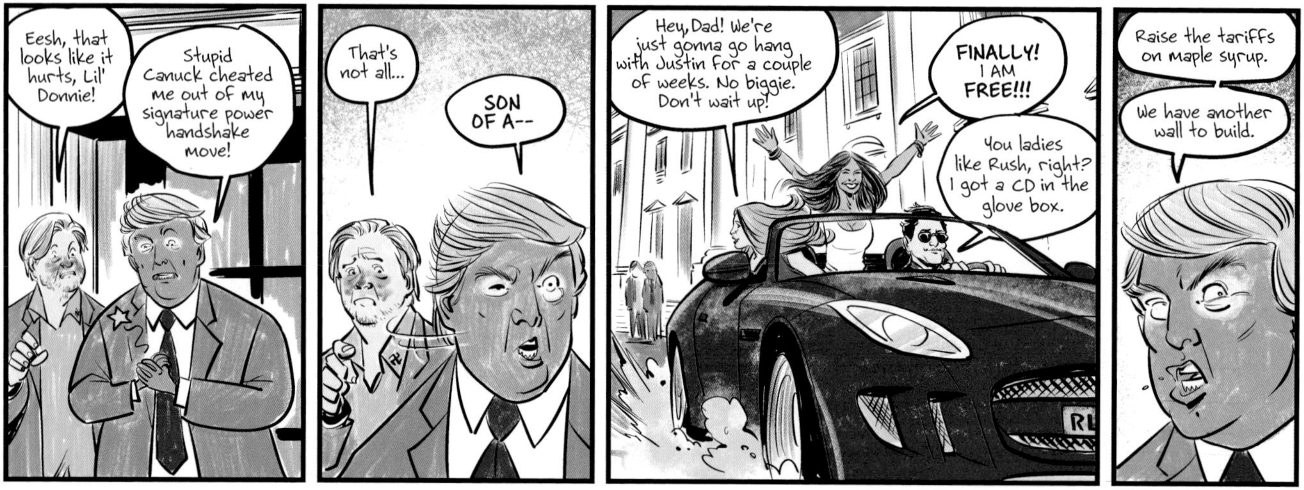

Eesh, that looks like it hurts, Lil' Donnie!
Stupid Canuck cheated me out of my signature power handshake move!
That's not all...
SON OF A--
Hey, Dad! We're just gonna go hang with Justin for a couple of weeks. No biggie. Don't wait up!
FINALLY! I AM FREE!!!
You ladies like Rush, right? I got a CD in the glove box.
Raise the tariffs on maple syrup.
We have another wall to build.

Feb 19, 2017

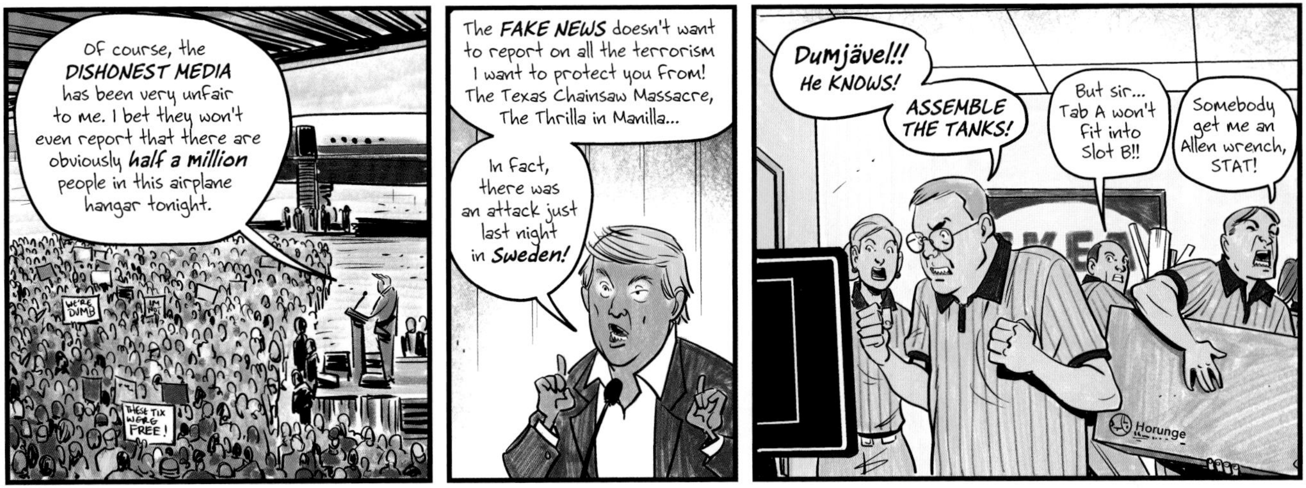
Of course, the DISHONEST MEDIA has been very unfair to me. I bet they won't even report that there are obviously half a million people in this airplane hangar tonight.
WE'RE DUMB
THESE TIX WERE FREE!
The FAKE NEWS doesn't want to report on all the terrorism I want to protect you from! The Texas Chainsaw Massacre, The Thrilla in Manilla...
In fact, there was an attack just last night in Sweden!
Dumjävel!! He KNOWS!
ASSEMBLE THE TANKS!
But sir... Tab A won't fit into Slot B!!
Somebody get me an Allen wrench, STAT!
Horunge

Feb 20, 2017

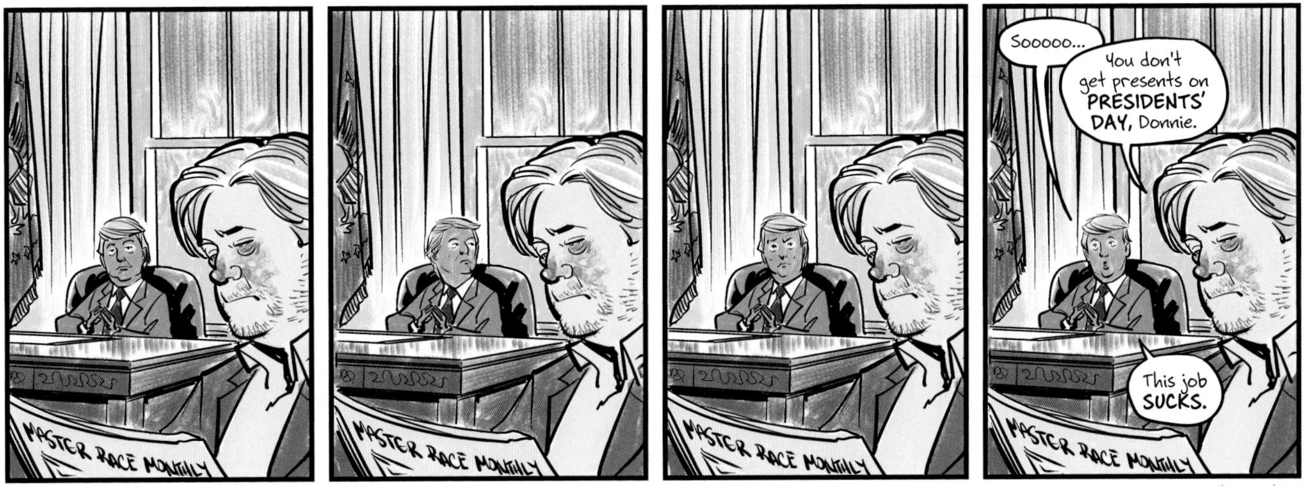
MASTER RACE MONTHLY
MASTER RACE MONTHLY
MASTER RACE MONTHLY
Soooooo...
You don't get presents on PRESIDENTS' DAY, Donnie.
This job SUCKS.
MASTER RACE MONTHLY

Feb 27, 2017

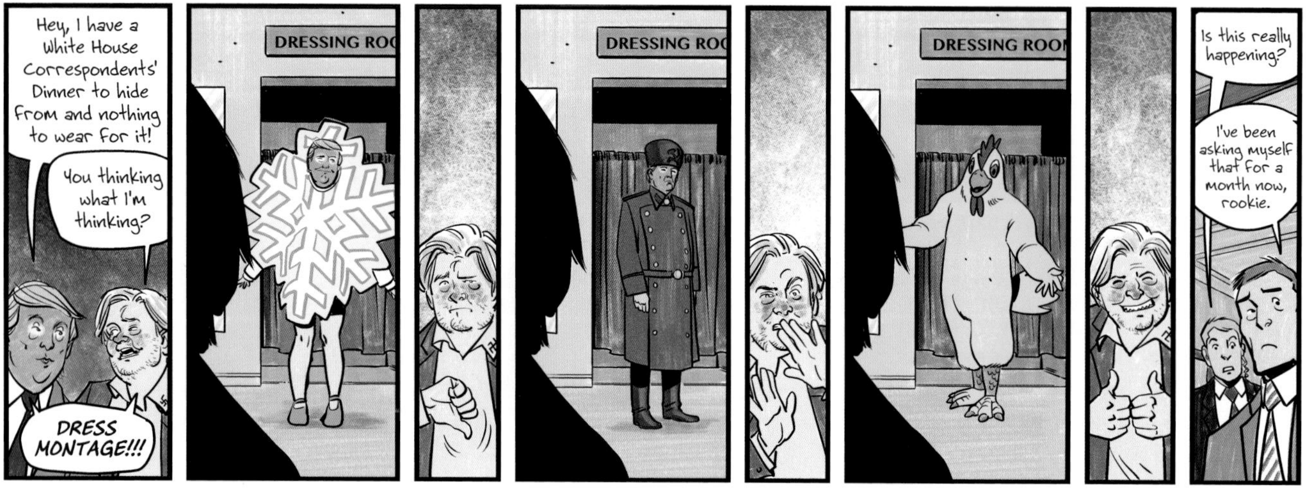
Hey, I have a White House Correspondents' Dinner to hide from and nothing to wear for it!
You thinking what I'm thinking?
DRESS MONTAGE!!!
DRESSING ROO
DRESSING ROO
DRESSING ROOM
Is this really happening?
I've been asking myself that for a month now, rookie.

Mar 1, 2017

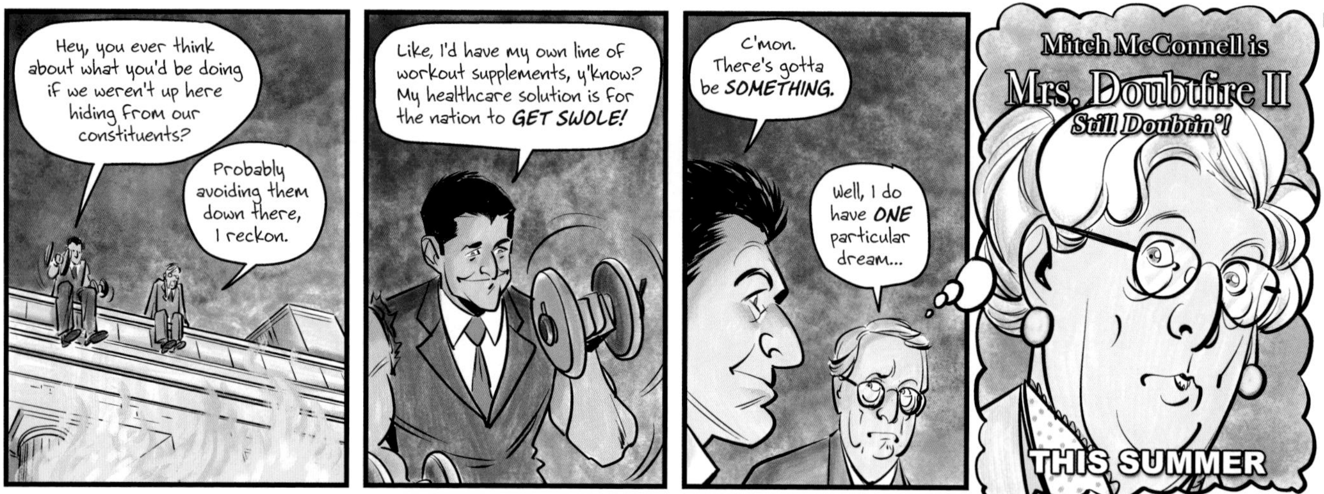
Hey, you ever think about what you'd be doing if we weren't up here hiding from our constituents?
Probably avoiding them down there, I reckon.
Like, I'd have my own line of workout supplements, y'know? My healthcare solution is for the nation to GET SWOLE!
C'mon. There's gotta be SOMETHING.
Well, I do have ONE particular dream...
Mitch McConnell is
Mrs. Doubtfire II
Still Doubtin'!
THIS SUMMER

Mar 9, 2017

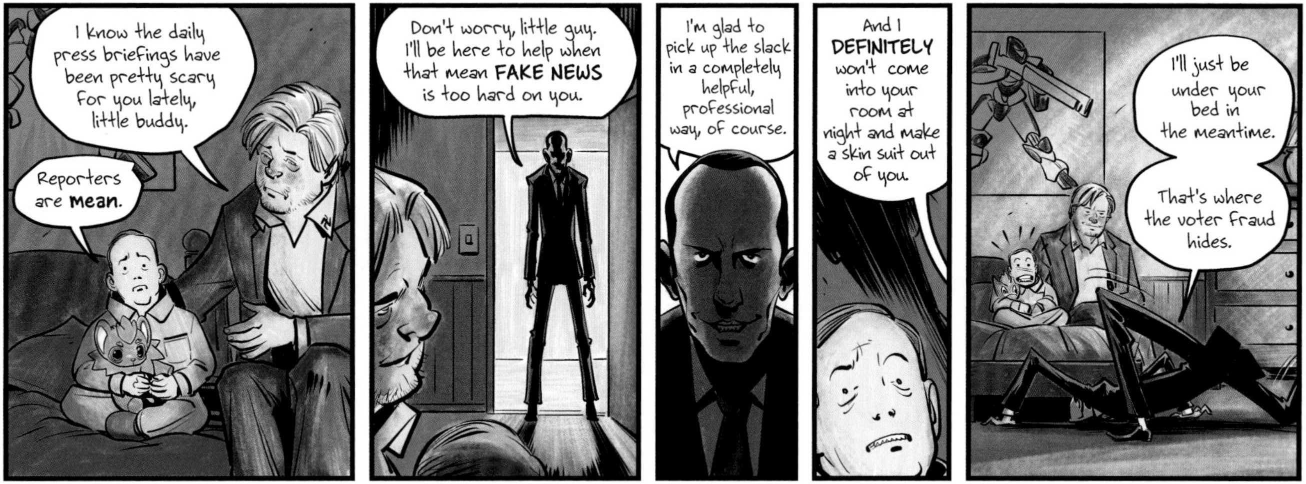
I know the daily press briefings have been pretty scary for you lately, little buddy.
Reporters are **mean**.
Don't worry, little guy. I'll be here to help when that mean **FAKE NEWS** is too hard on you.
I'm glad to pick up the slack in a completely helpful, professional way, of course.
And I **DEFINITELY** won't come into your room at night and make a skin suit out of you.
I'll just be under your bed in the meantime.
That's where the voter fraud hides.

Mar 13, 2017

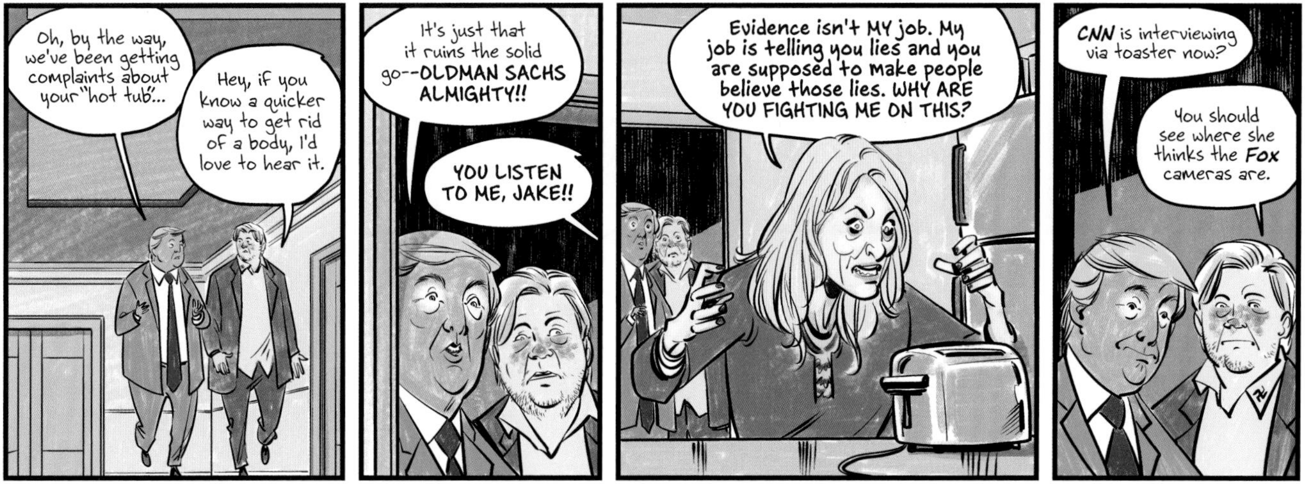
Oh, by the way, we've been getting complaints about your "hot tub"...
Hey, if you know a quicker way to get rid of a body, I'd love to hear it.
It's just that it ruins the solid go--OLDMAN SACHS ALMIGHTY!!
YOU LISTEN TO ME, JAKE!!
Evidence isn't MY job. My job is telling you lies and you are supposed to make people believe those lies. WHY ARE YOU FIGHTING ME ON THIS?
CNN is interviewing via toaster now?
You should see where she thinks the **Fox** cameras are.

Lil' Donnie

by Mike Norton

May 14, 2017

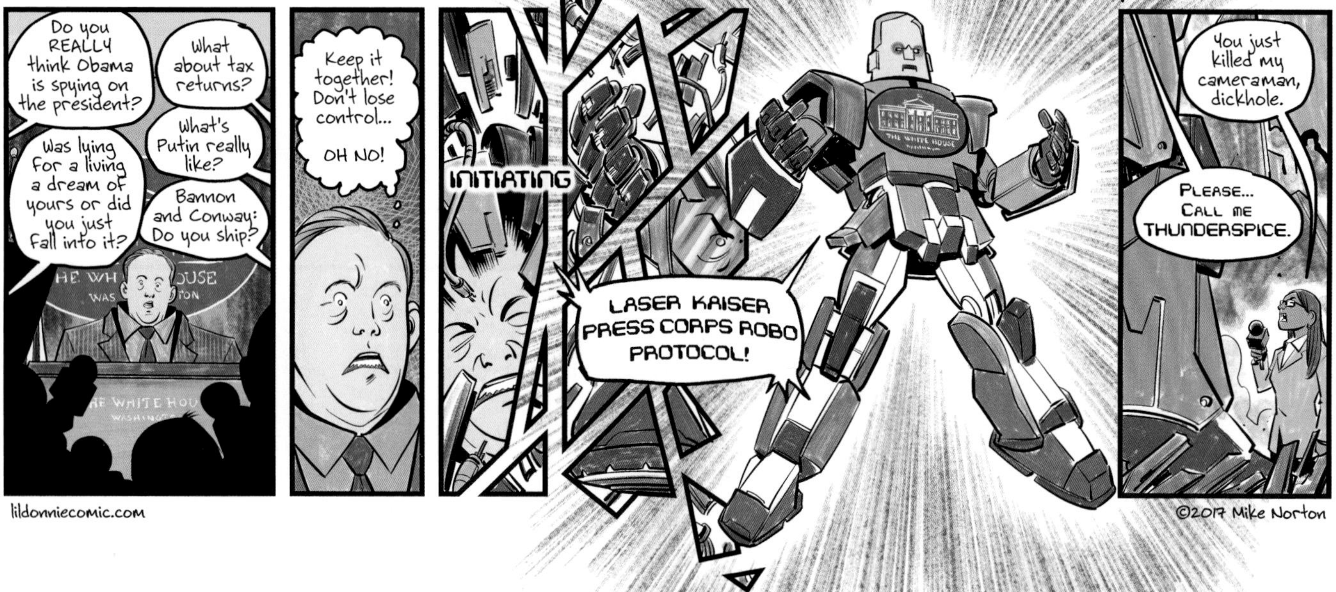
Do you REALLY think Obama is spying on the president?
What about tax returns?
Was lying for a living a dream of yours or did you just fall into it?
What's Putin really like?
Bannon and Conway: Do you ship?
Keep it together! Don't lose control...
OH NO!
INITIATING
LASER KAISER PRESS CORPS ROBO PROTOCOL!
You just killed my cameraman, dickhole.
PLEASE... CALL ME THUNDERSPICE.

lildonniecomic.com

Mar 17, 2017

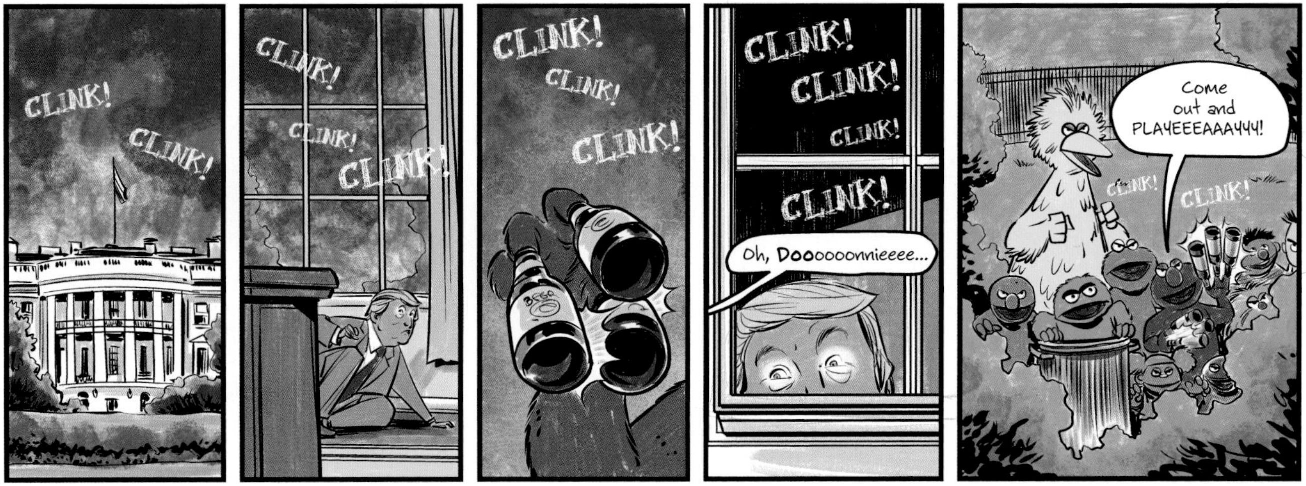
CLINK!
CLINK!
CLINK!
CLINK!
CLINK!
CLINK!
CLINK!
CLINK!
CLINK!
CLINK!
CLINK!
CLINK!
Oh, Doooooonnieeee...
CLINK!
CLINK!
Come out and PLAYEEEAAAYYY!

Mar 20, 2017

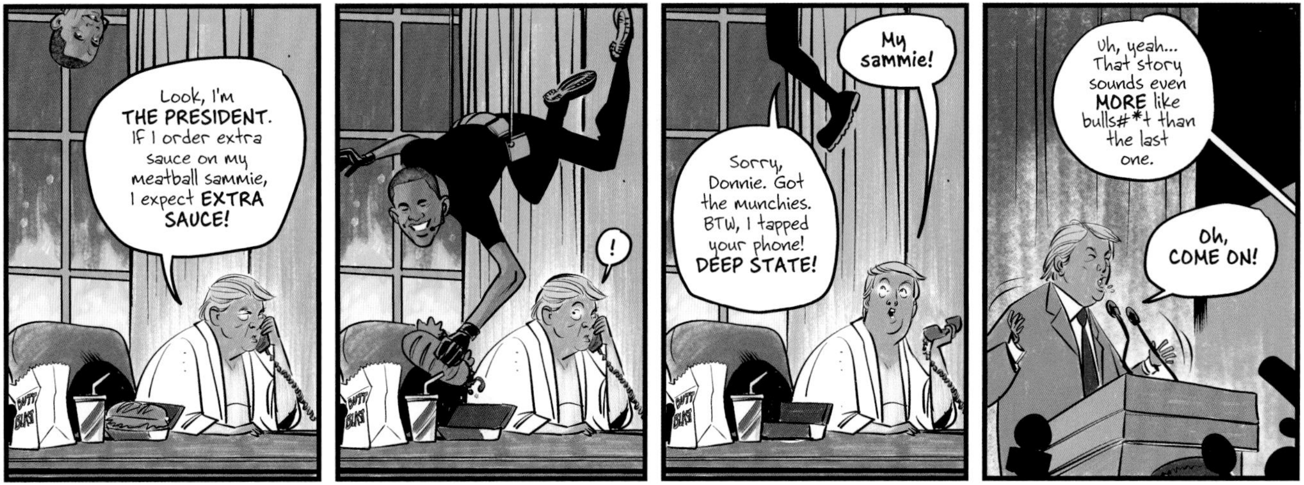
Look, I'm THE PRESIDENT. If I order extra sauce on my meatball sammie, I expect EXTRA SAUCE!
!
Sorry, Donnie. Got the munchies. BTW, I tapped your phone! DEEP STATE!
My sammie!
Uh, yeah... That story sounds even MORE like bulls#*t than the last one.
Oh, COME ON!

Mar 21, 2017

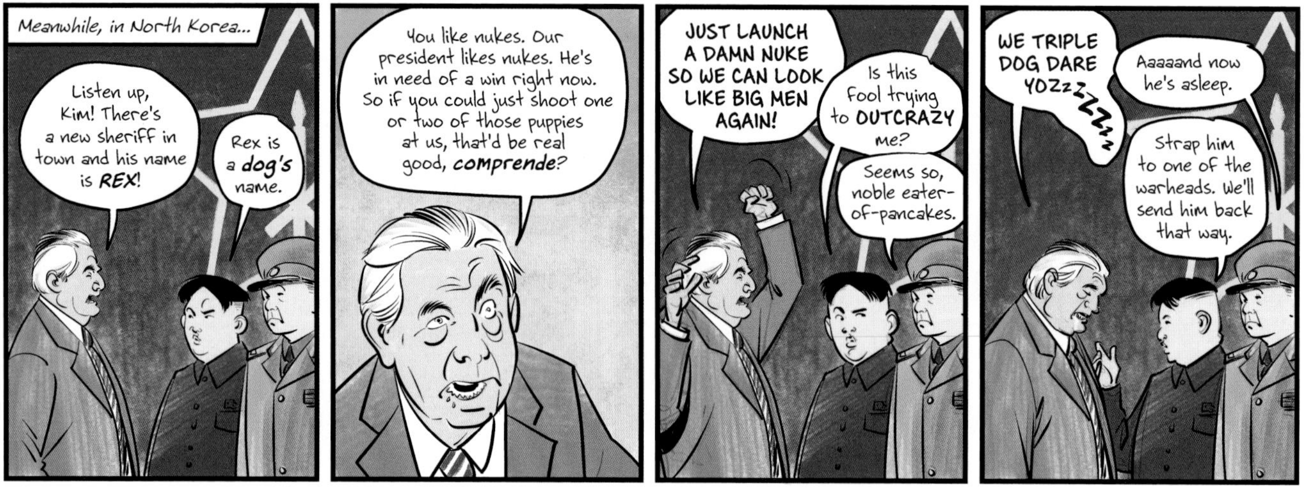
Meanwhile, in North Korea...
Listen up, Kim! There's a new sheriff in town and his name is **REX**!
Rex is a **dog's** name.
You like nukes. Our president likes nukes. He's in need of a win right now. So if you could just shoot one or two of those puppies at us, that'd be real good, **comprende**?
JUST LAUNCH A DAMN NUKE SO WE CAN LOOK LIKE BIG MEN AGAIN!
Is this fool trying to **OUTCRAZY** me?
Seems so, noble eater-of-pancakes.
WE TRIPLE DOG DARE YOZzzZZZzz
Aaaaand now he's asleep.
Strap him to one of the warheads. We'll send him back that way.

Mar 22, 2017

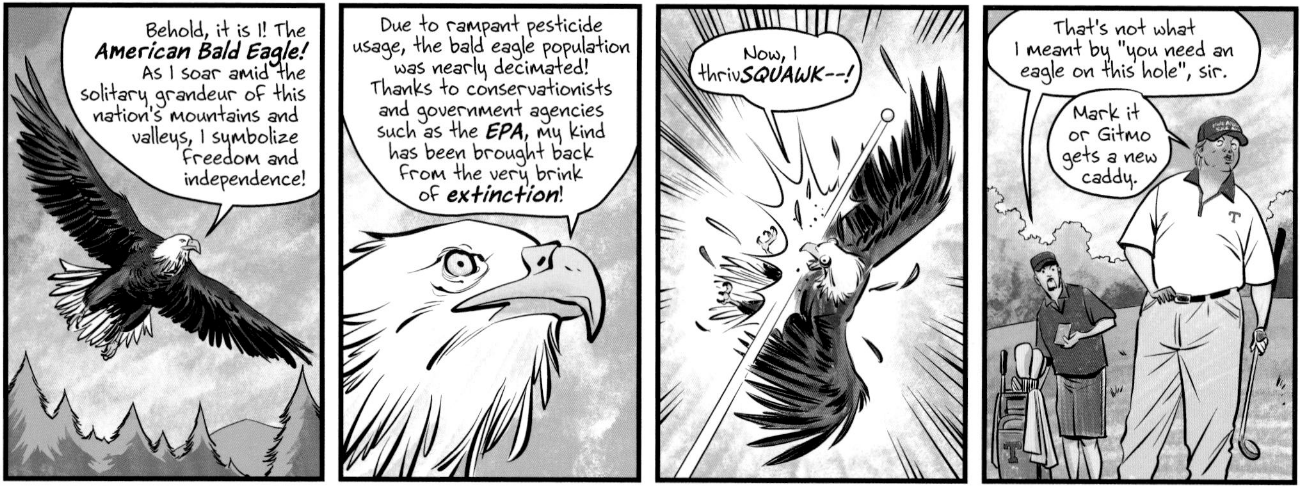
Behold, it is I! The **American Bald Eagle!** As I soar amid the solitary grandeur of this nation's mountains and valleys, I symbolize freedom and independence!
Due to rampant pesticide usage, the bald eagle population was nearly decimated! Thanks to conservationists and government agencies such as the **EPA**, my kind has been brought back from the very brink of **extinction**!
Now, I thriv**SQUAWK**--!
That's not what I meant by "you need an eagle on this hole", sir.
Mark it or Gitmo gets a new caddy.

Mar 24, 2017

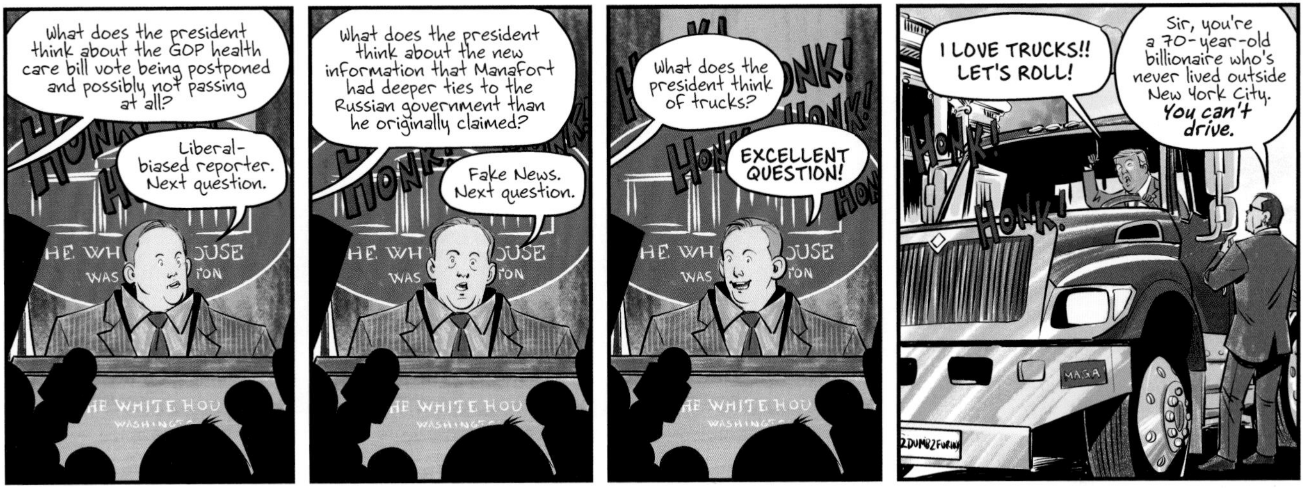
What does the president think about the GOP health care bill vote being postponed and possibly not passing at all?
Liberal-biased reporter. Next question.
What does the president think about the new information that Manafort had deeper ties to the Russian government than he originally claimed?
Fake News. Next question.
What does the president think of trucks?
EXCELLENT QUESTION!
HONK!
I LOVE TRUCKS!! LET'S ROLL!
Sir, you're a 70-year-old billionaire who's never lived outside New York City. You can't drive.
MAGA

Mar 27, 2017

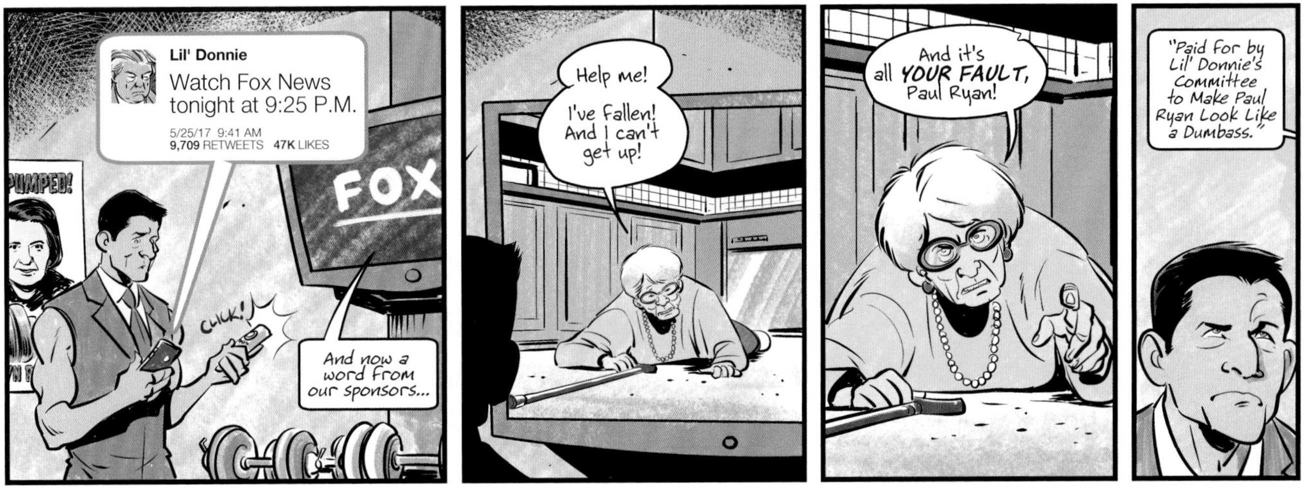
Lil' Donnie
Watch Fox News tonight at 9:25 P.M.
5/25/17 9:41 AM
9,709 RETWEETS 47K LIKES
PUMPED!
FOX
CLICK!
And now a word from our sponsors...
Help me!
I've fallen! And I can't get up!
And it's all YOUR FAULT, Paul Ryan!
"Paid for by Lil' Donnie's Committee to Make Paul Ryan Look Like a Dumbass."

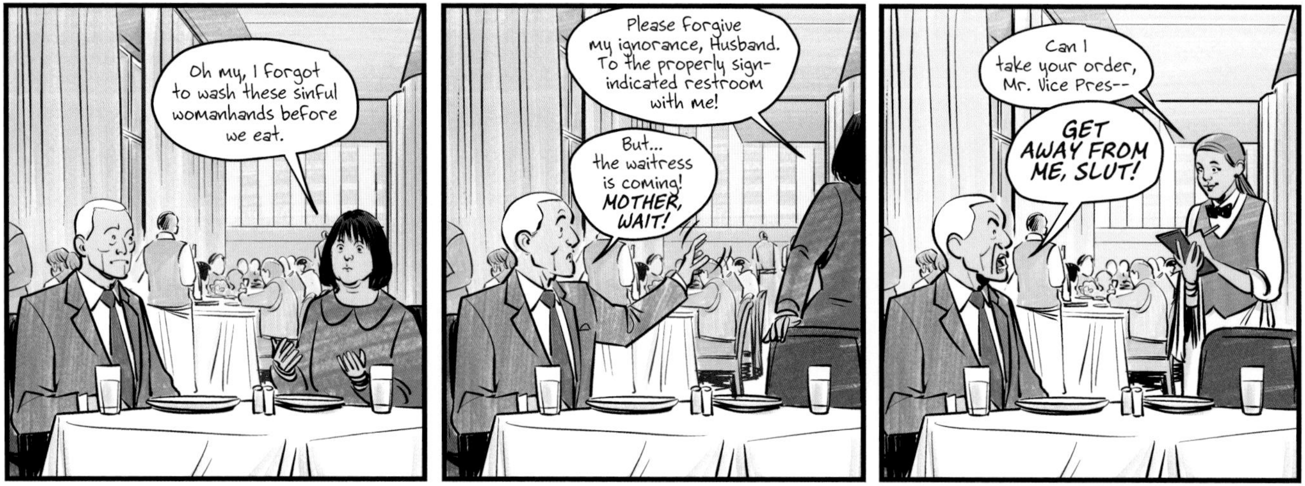
Oh my, I forgot to wash these sinful womanhands before we eat.
Please forgive my ignorance, Husband. To the properly sign-indicated restroom with me!
But... the waitress is coming! **MOTHER, WAIT!**
Can I take your order, Mr. Vice Pres--
GET AWAY FROM ME, SLUT!

Mar 31, 2017

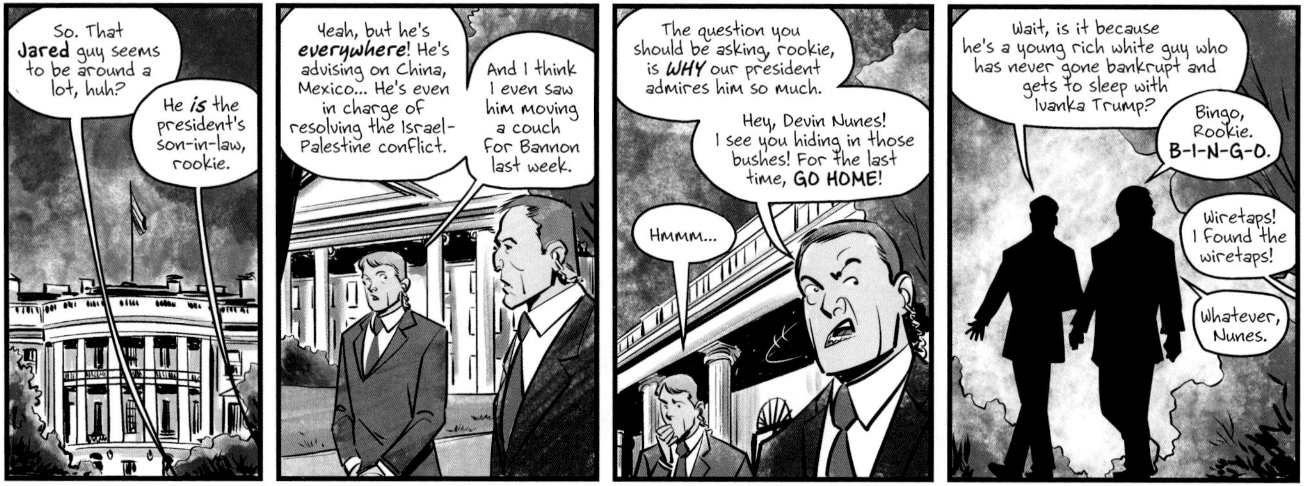
So. That **Jared** guy seems to be around a lot, huh?
He ***is*** the president's son-in-law, rookie.
Yeah, but he's ***everywhere***! He's advising on China, Mexico... He's even in charge of resolving the Israel-Palestine conflict.
And I think I even saw him moving a couch for Bannon last week.
The question you should be asking, rookie, is ***WHY*** our president admires him so much.
Hey, Devin Nunes! I see you hiding in those bushes! For the last time, **GO HOME**!
Hmmm...
Wait, is it because he's a young rich white guy who has never gone bankrupt and gets to sleep with Ivanka Trump?
Bingo, Rookie. **B-I-N-G-O.**
Wiretaps! I found the wiretaps!
Whatever, Nunes.

Apr 3, 2017

Apr 6, 2017

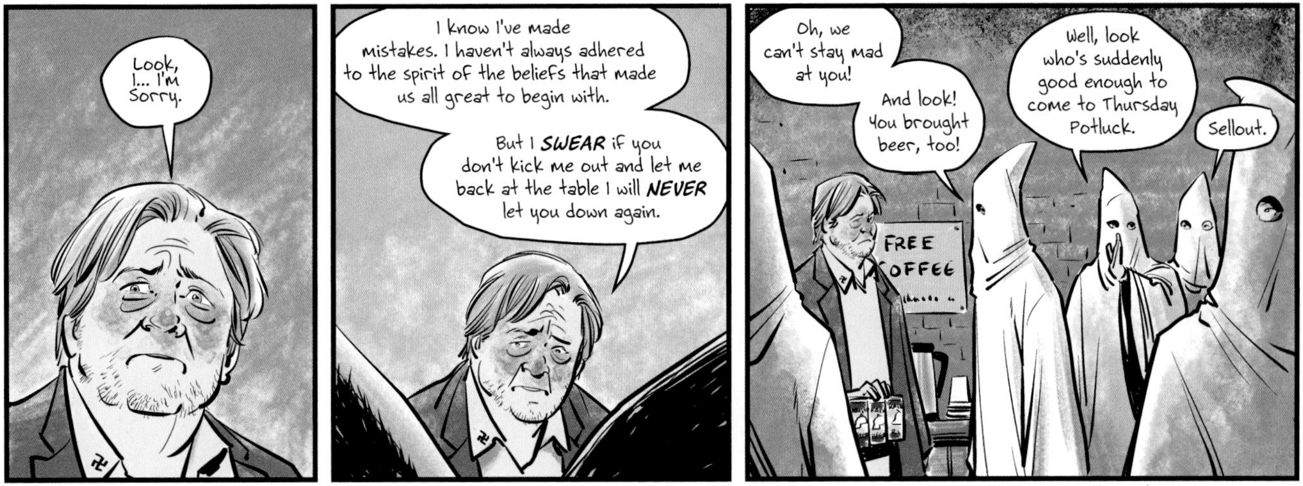
Look, I... I'm Sorry.
I know I've made mistakes. I haven't always adhered to the spirit of the beliefs that made us all great to begin with.
But I **SWEAR** if you don't kick me out and let me back at the table I will **NEVER** let you down again.
Oh, we can't stay mad at you!
And look! You brought beer, too!
Well, look who's suddenly good enough to come to Thursday Potluck.
Sellout.
FREE COFFEE

Apr 7, 2017

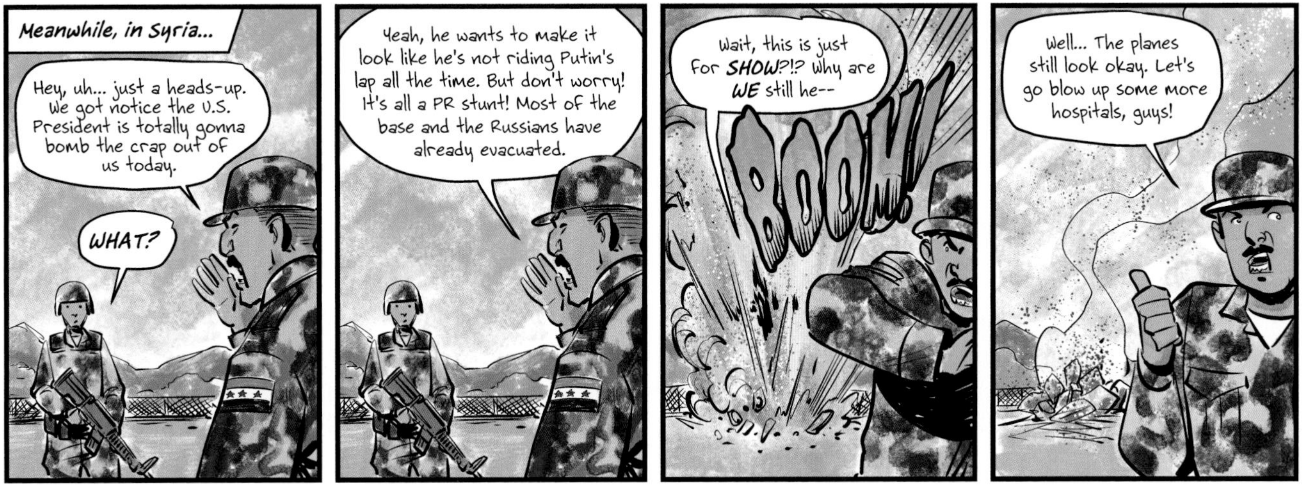
Meanwhile, in Syria...
Hey, uh... just a heads-up. We got notice the U.S. President is totally gonna bomb the crap out of us today.
WHAT?
Yeah, he wants to make it look like he's not riding Putin's lap all the time. But don't worry! It's all a PR stunt! Most of the base and the Russians have already evacuated.
Wait, this is just for **SHOW**?!? Why are **WE** still he--
BOOM!
Well... The planes still look okay. Let's go blow up some more hospitals, guys!

Apr 10, 2017

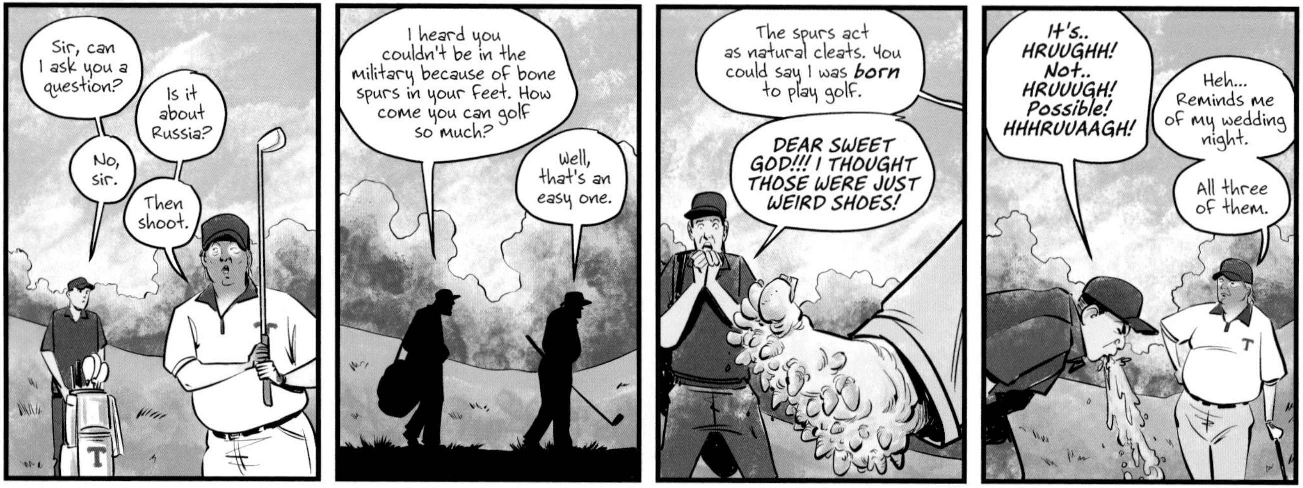
Sir, can I ask you a question?
Is it about Russia?
No, sir.
Then shoot.
I heard you couldn't be in the military because of bone spurs in your feet. How come you can golf so much?
Well, that's an easy one.
The spurs act as natural cleats. You could say I was born to play golf.
DEAR SWEET GOD!!! I THOUGHT THOSE WERE JUST WEIRD SHOES!
It's.. HRUUGHH! Not.. HRUUUGH! Possible! HHHRUUAAGH!
Heh... Reminds me of my wedding night.
All three of them.

Apr 12, 2017

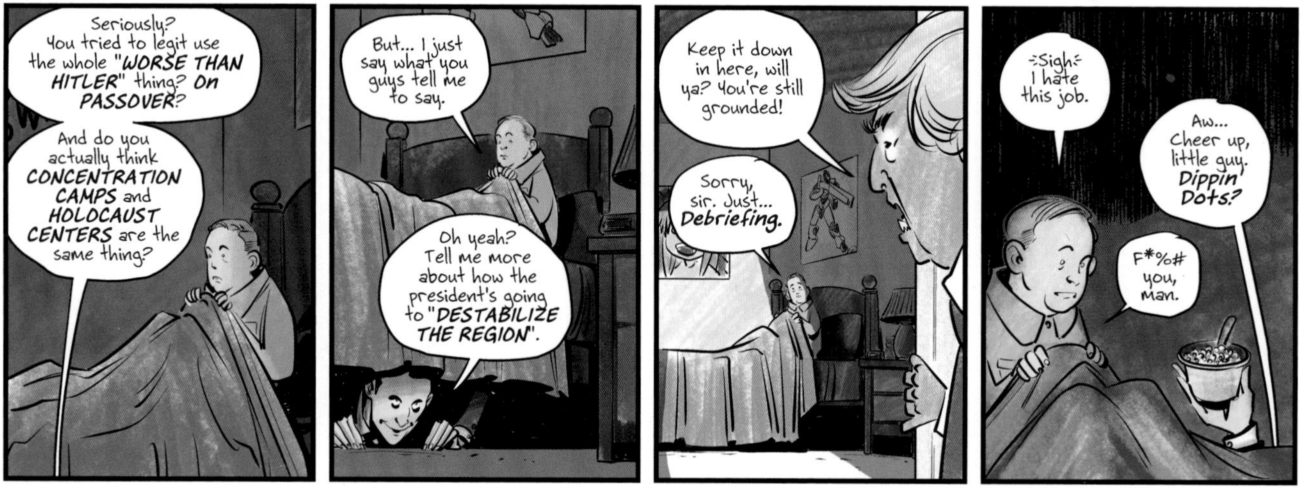
Seriously? You tried to legit use the whole "WORSE THAN HITLER" thing? On PASSOVER?
And do you actually think CONCENTRATION CAMPS and HOLOCAUST CENTERS are the same thing?
But... I just say what you guys tell me to say.
Oh yeah? Tell me more about how the president's going to "DESTABILIZE THE REGION".
Keep it down in here, will ya? You're still grounded!
Sorry, sir. Just... Debriefing.
:Sigh: I hate this job.
Aw... Cheer up, little guy. Dippin' Dots?
F*%# you, man.

Apr 14, 2017

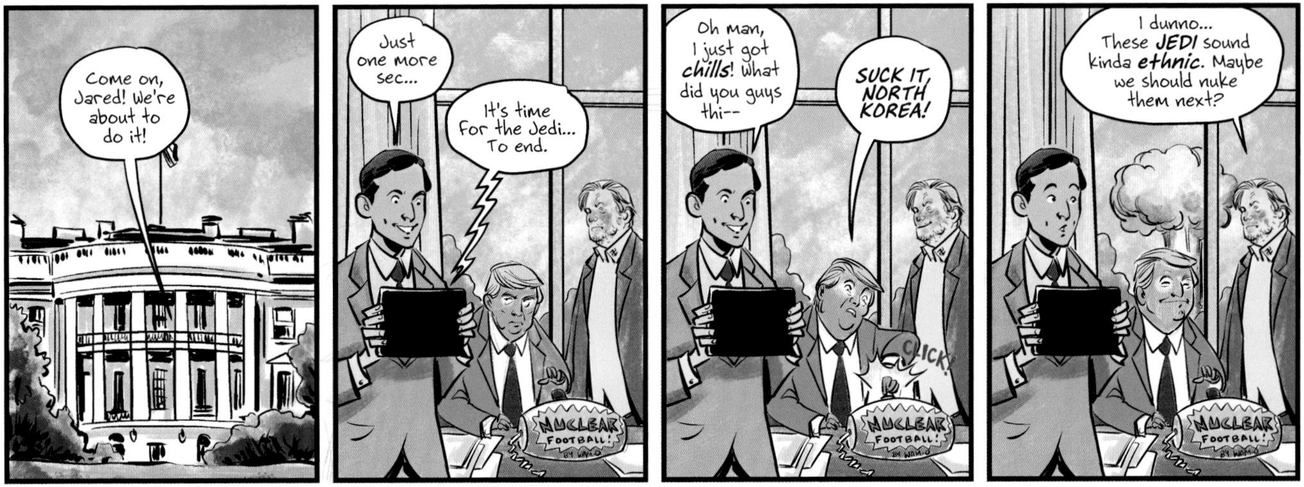
Come on, Jared! We're about to do it!
Just one more sec...
It's time for the Jedi... To end.
NUCLEAR FOOTBALL!
Oh man, I just got **chills**! What did you guys thi--
SUCK IT, NORTH KOREA!
CLICK!
NUCLEAR FOOTBALL!
I dunno... These **JEDI** sound kinda **ethnic**. Maybe we should nuke them next?
NUCLEAR FOOTBALL!

Apr 17, 2017

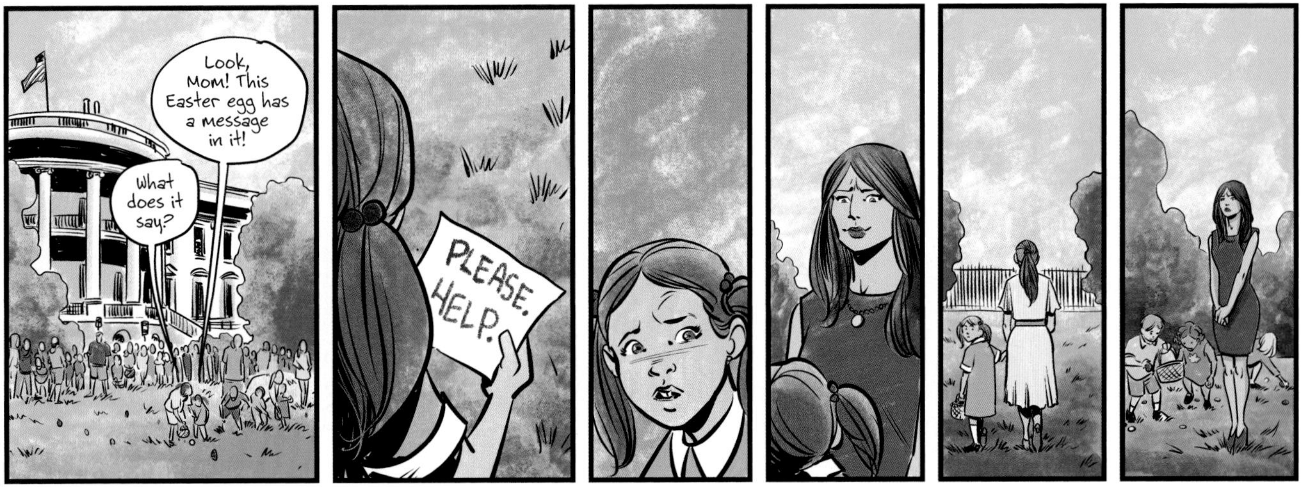
Look, Mom! This Easter egg has a message in it!
What does it say?
PLEASE. HELP.

Apr 24, 2017

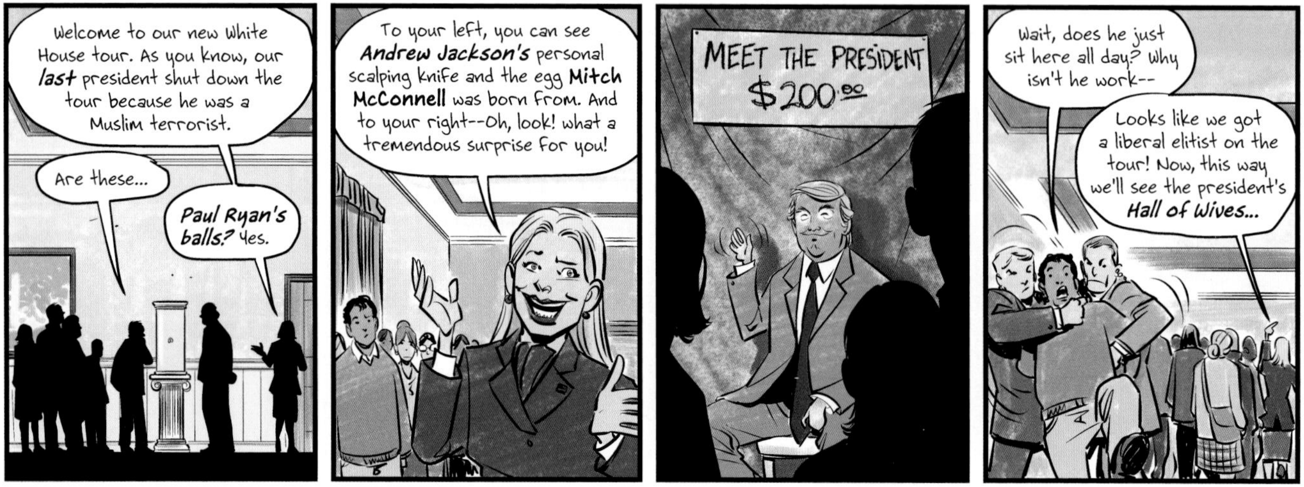

Welcome to our new White House tour. As you know, our **last** president shut down the tour because he was a Muslim terrorist.
Are these...
Paul Ryan's balls? Yes.
To your left, you can see **Andrew Jackson's** personal scalping knife and the egg **Mitch McConnell** was born from. And to your right--Oh, look! what a tremendous surprise for you!
MEET THE PRESIDENT $200.00
Wait, does he just sit here all day? Why isn't he work--
Looks like we got a liberal elitist on the tour! Now, this way we'll see the president's **Hall of Wives...**

Apr 26, 2017

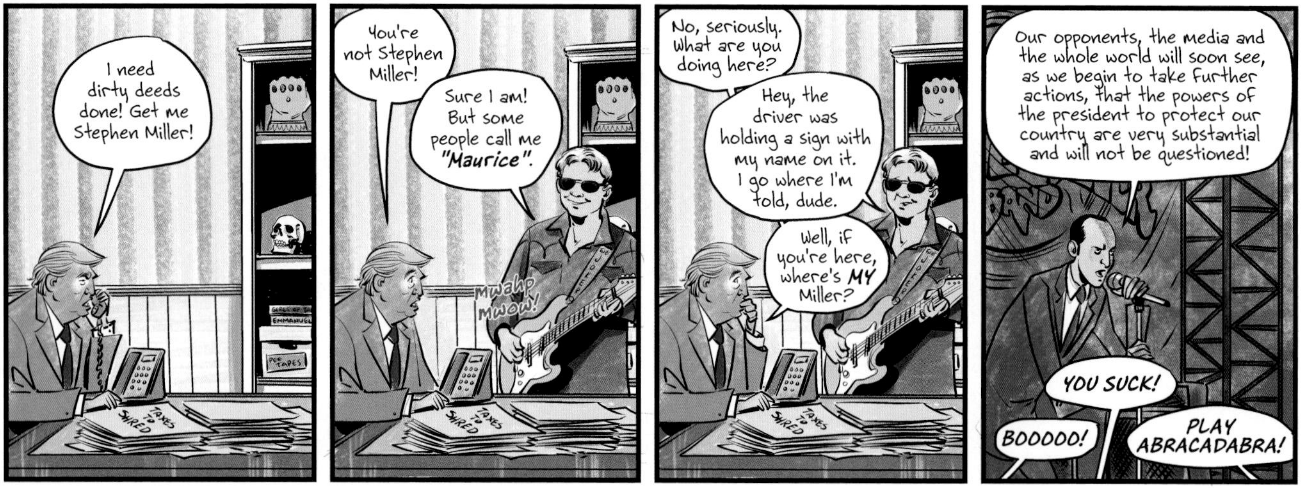

I need dirty deeds done! Get me Stephen Miller!
You're not Stephen Miller!
Sure I am! But some people call me **"Maurice"**.
MWAHP MWOW!
No, seriously. What are you doing here?
Hey, the driver was holding a sign with my name on it. I go where I'm told, dude.
Well, if you're here, where's **MY** Miller?
Our opponents, the media and the whole world will soon see, as we begin to take further actions, that the powers of the president to protect our country are very substantial and will not be questioned!
YOU SUCK!
BOOOOO!
PLAY ABRACADABRA!

May 1, 2017

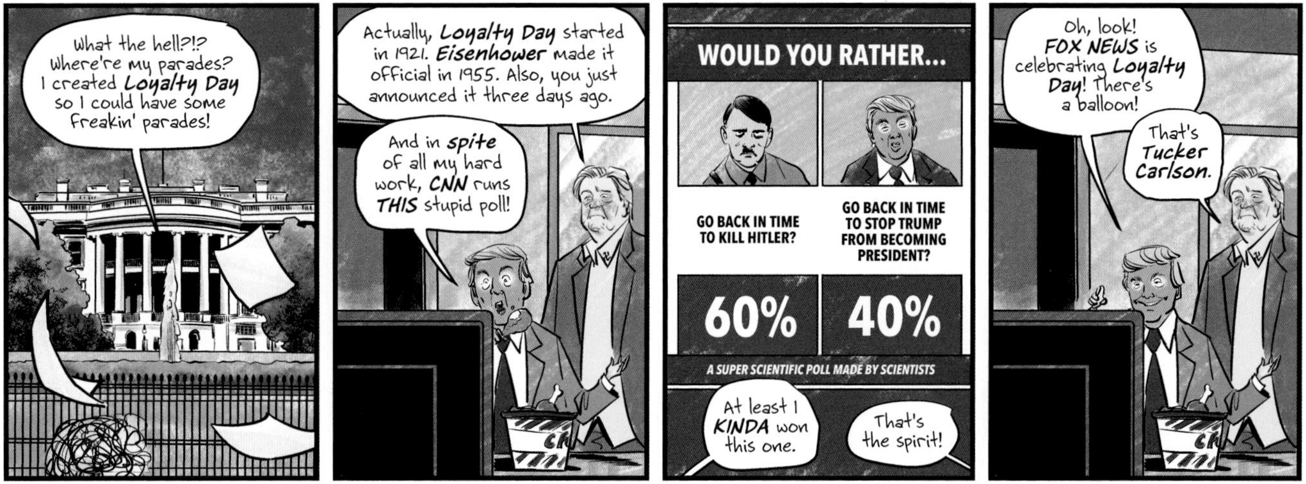

May 3, 2017

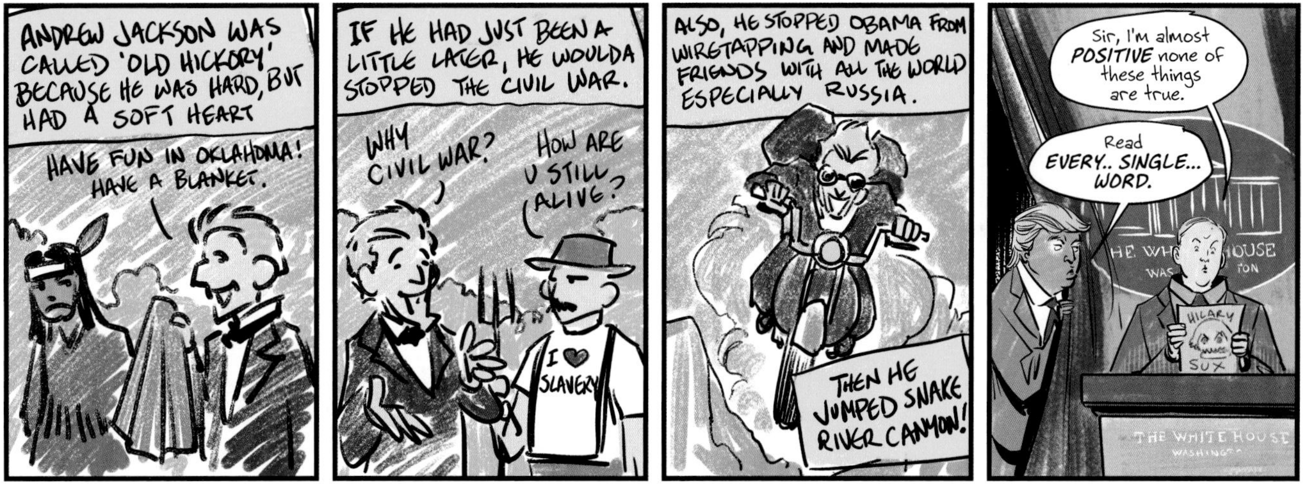

May 8, 2017

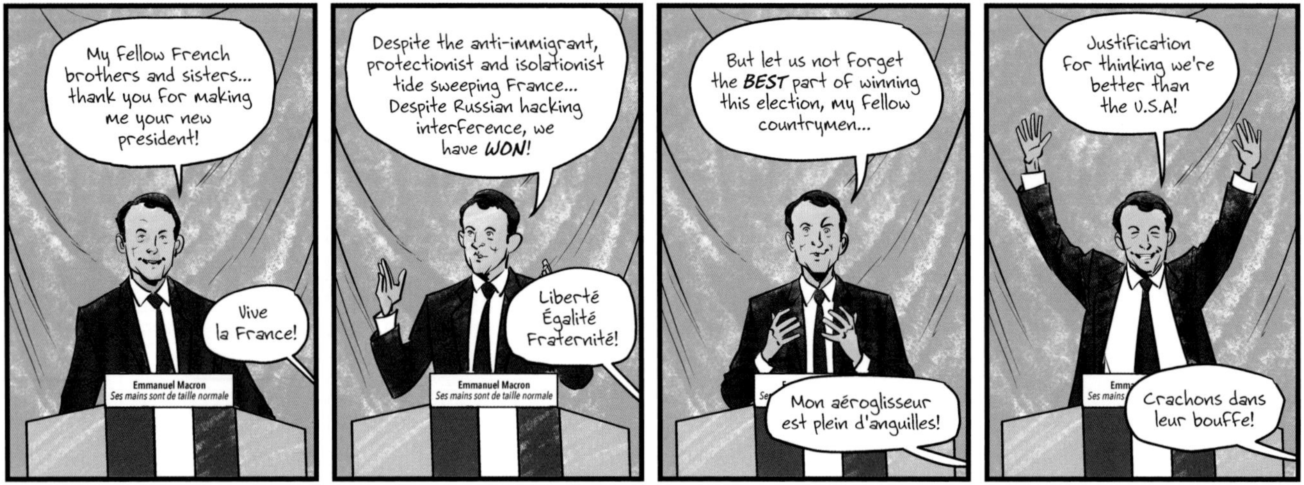
My fellow French brothers and sisters... thank you for making me your new president!
Vive la France!
Emmanuel Macron
Ses mains sont de taille normale
Despite the anti-immigrant, protectionist and isolationist tide sweeping France... Despite Russian hacking interference, we have **WON**!
Liberté Égalité Fraternité!
Emmanuel Macron
Ses mains sont de taille normale
But let us not forget the **BEST** part of winning this election, my fellow countrymen...
Mon aéroglisseur est plein d'anguilles!
Justification for thinking we're better than the U.S.A!
Crachons dans leur bouffe!

May 10, 2017

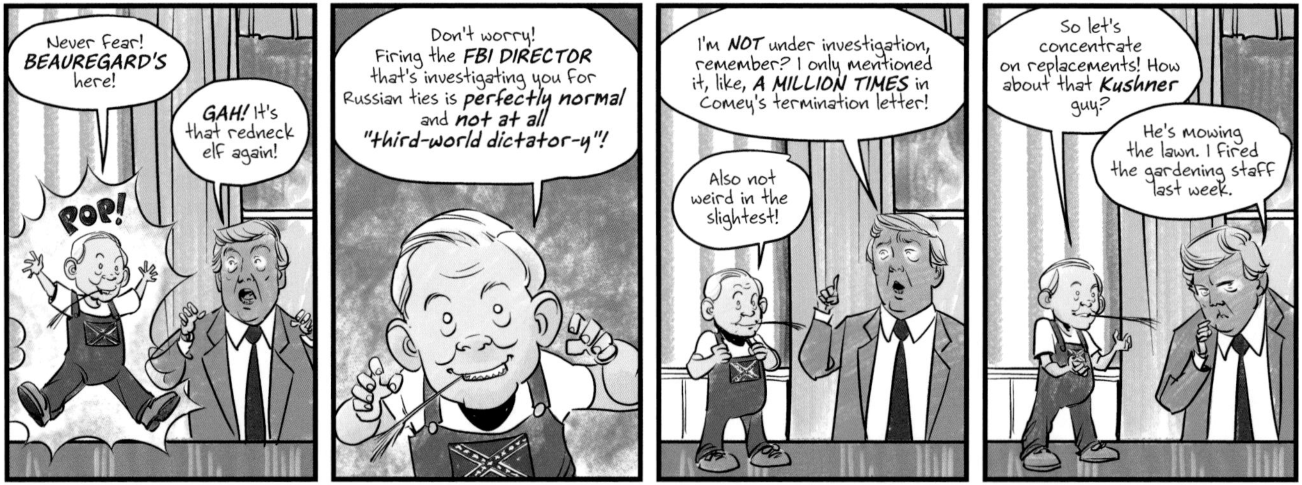
Never fear! **BEAUREGARD'S** here!
POP!
GAH! It's that redneck elf again!
Don't worry! Firing the **FBI DIRECTOR** that's investigating you for Russian ties is ***perfectly normal*** and ***not at all*** ***"third-world dictator-y"***!
I'm **NOT** under investigation, remember? I only mentioned it, like, **A MILLION TIMES** in Comey's termination letter!
Also not weird in the slightest!
So let's concentrate on replacements! How about that ***Kushner*** guy?
He's mowing the lawn. I fired the gardening staff last week.

May 11, 2017

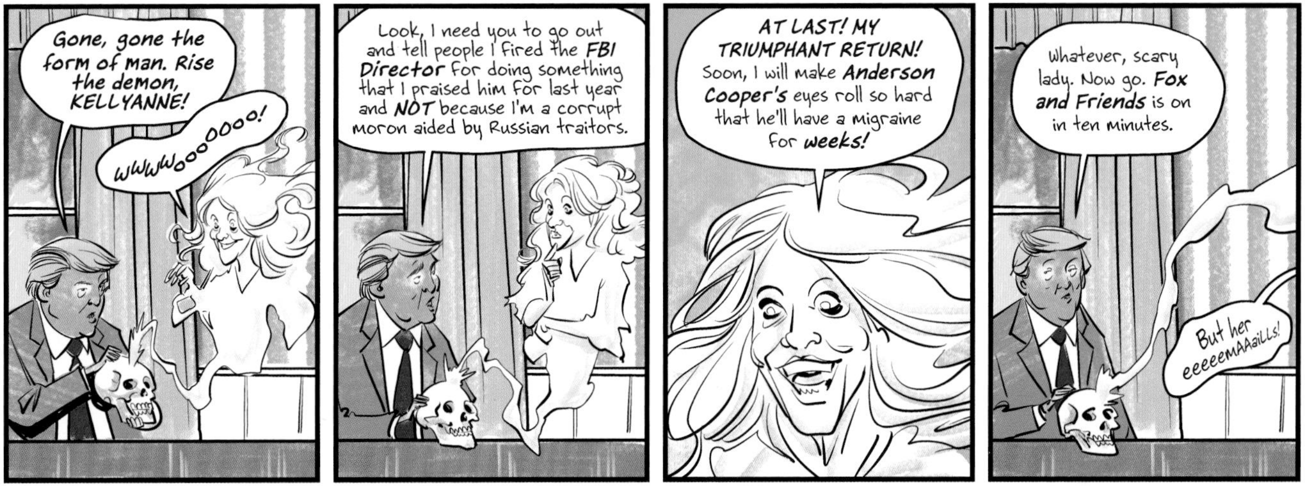
Gone, gone the form of man. Rise the demon, KELLYANNE!
WWWWooooOOOO!
Look, I need you to go out and tell people I fired the FBI Director for doing something that I praised him for last year and NOT because I'm a corrupt moron aided by Russian traitors.
AT LAST! MY TRIUMPHANT RETURN! Soon, I will make Anderson Cooper's eyes roll so hard that he'll have a migraine for weeks!
Whatever, scary lady. Now go. Fox and Friends is on in ten minutes.
But her eeeeeMAAaiLLs!

May 12, 2017

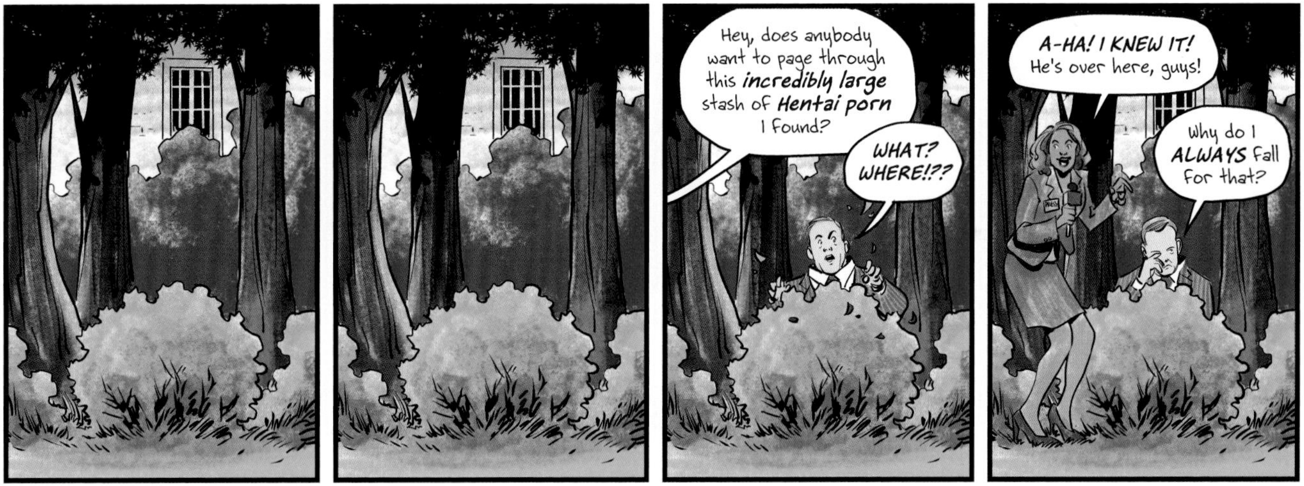
Hey, does anybody want to page through this incredibly large stash of Hentai porn I found?
WHAT? WHERE!??
A-HA! I KNEW IT! He's over here, guys!
Why do I ALWAYS fall for that?

May 16, 2017

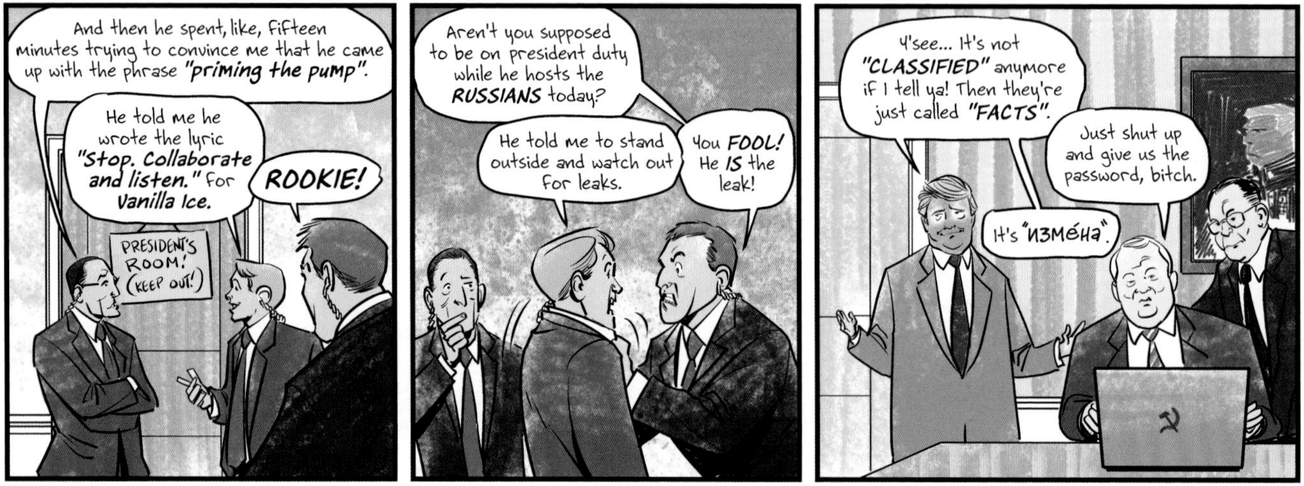

And then he spent, like, fifteen minutes trying to convince me that he came up with the phrase **"priming the pump"**.
He told me he wrote the lyric **"Stop. Collaborate and listen."** for **Vanilla Ice.**
ROOKIE!
PRESIDENT'S ROOM! (KEEP OUT!)
Aren't you supposed to be on president duty while he hosts the **RUSSIANS** today?
He told me to stand outside and watch out for leaks.
You **FOOL!** He **IS** the leak!
Y'see... It's not **"CLASSIFIED"** anymore if I tell ya! Then they're just called **"FACTS"**.
Just shut up and give us the password, bitch.
It's "ИЗМЕ́НА".

May 18, 2017

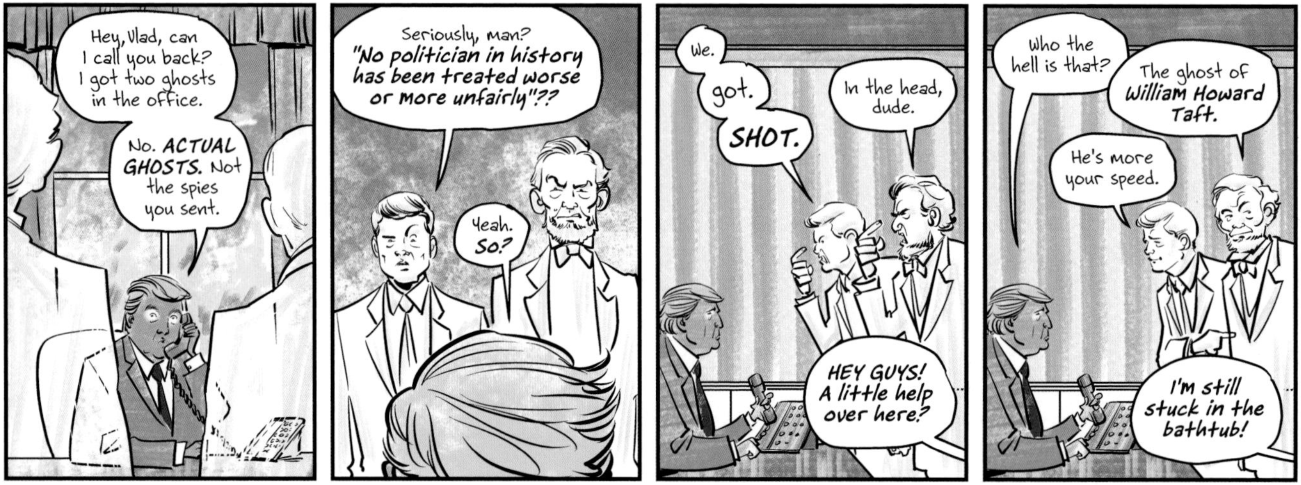

Hey, Vlad, can I call you back? I got two ghosts in the office.
No. **ACTUAL GHOSTS.** Not the spies you sent.
Seriously, man? ***"No politician in history has been treated worse or more unfairly"??***
Yeah. **So?**
We.
got.
SHOT.
In the head, dude.
HEY GUYS! A little help over here?
Who the hell is that?
The ghost of **William Howard Taft.**
He's more your speed.
I'm still stuck in the bathtub!

May 22, 2017

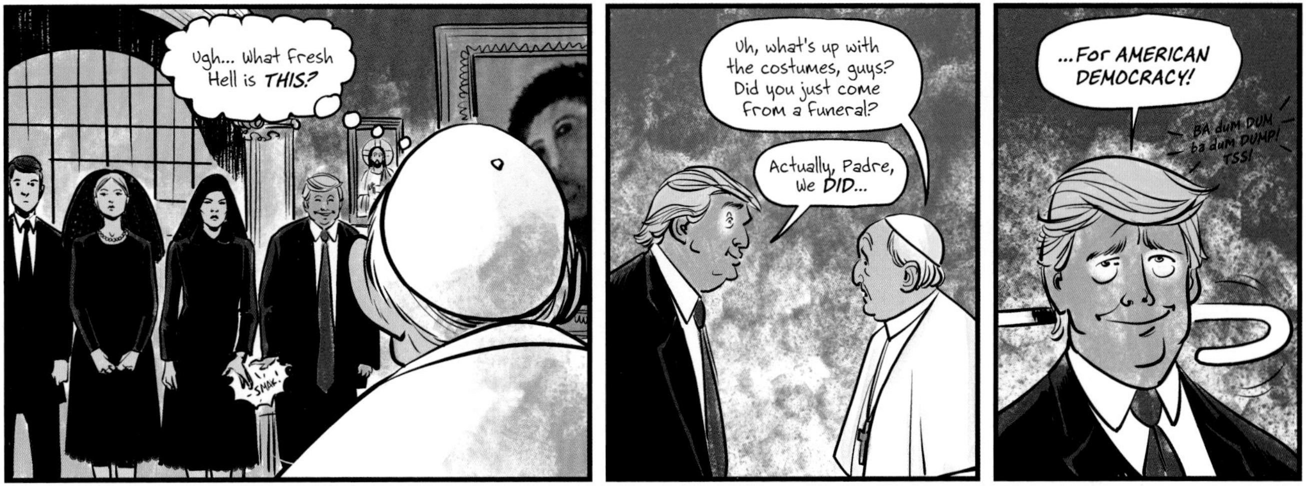

Ugh... What Fresh Hell is THIS?
SMAK!
Uh, what's up with the costumes, guys? Did you just come from a funeral?
Actually, Padre, we DID...
...For AMERICAN DEMOCRACY!
BA dum DUM ba dum DUMP! TSS!

May 22, 2017

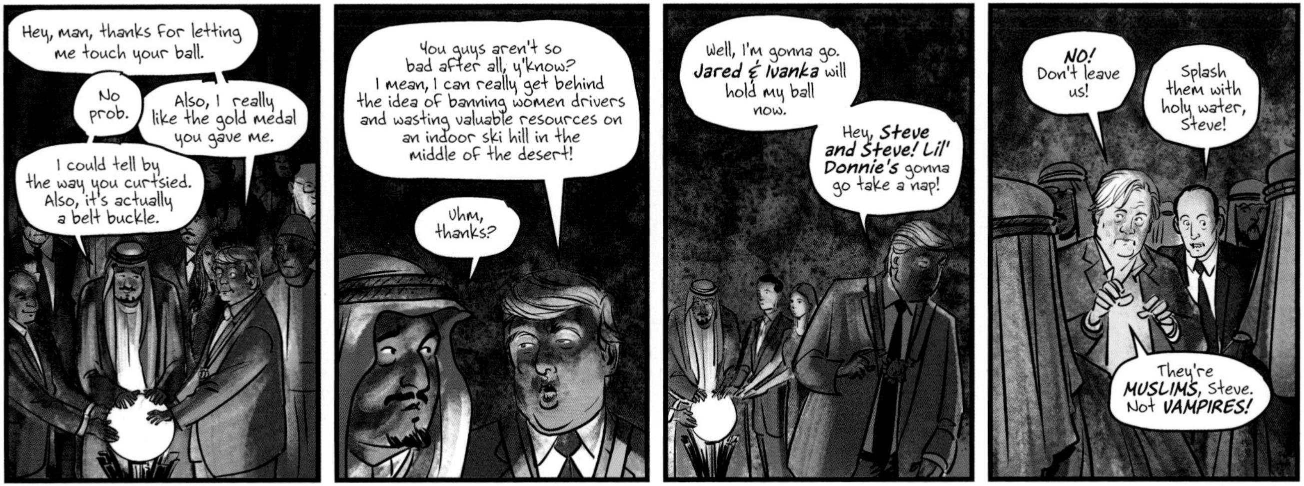

Hey, man, thanks for letting me touch your ball.
No prob.
Also, I really like the gold medal you gave me.
I could tell by the way you curtsied. Also, it's actually a belt buckle.
You guys aren't so bad after all, y'know? I mean, I can really get behind the idea of banning women drivers and wasting valuable resources on an indoor ski hill in the middle of the desert!
Uhm, thanks?
Well, I'm gonna go. Jared & Ivanka will hold my ball now.
Hey, Steve and Steve! Lil' Donnie's gonna go take a nap!
NO! Don't leave us!
Splash them with holy water, Steve!
They're MUSLIMS, Steve. Not VAMPIRES!

May 26, 2017

Lil' Donnie

by Mike Norton

Meanwhile, in Montana...
I am the cream in the World Wrestling Federation and there is no doubt about it, yeah, you, Mean Gene Okerlund, you know that I'm the cream of the crop!
MONTANA
"We let bears vote, too!"
I'm talking about all the way to the top, yeah. I'm justifiably in a position that I'd rather not be in. But the cream will rise to the top, ooh yeah!
Sir, can I get in a question about the AHCA? GRRK!
MONTANA
"We let bears vote, too!"
GIANT FORT! GIANT FORT!!
SLAM!
CRASH!
Ladies and gentlemen, I believe we have a new Press Secretary!
sigh I'll pack my stuff.

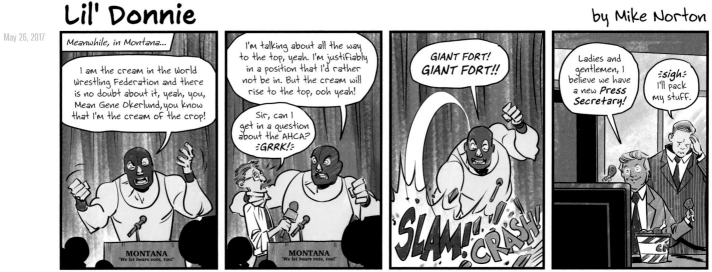

lildonniecomic.com

May 29, 2017

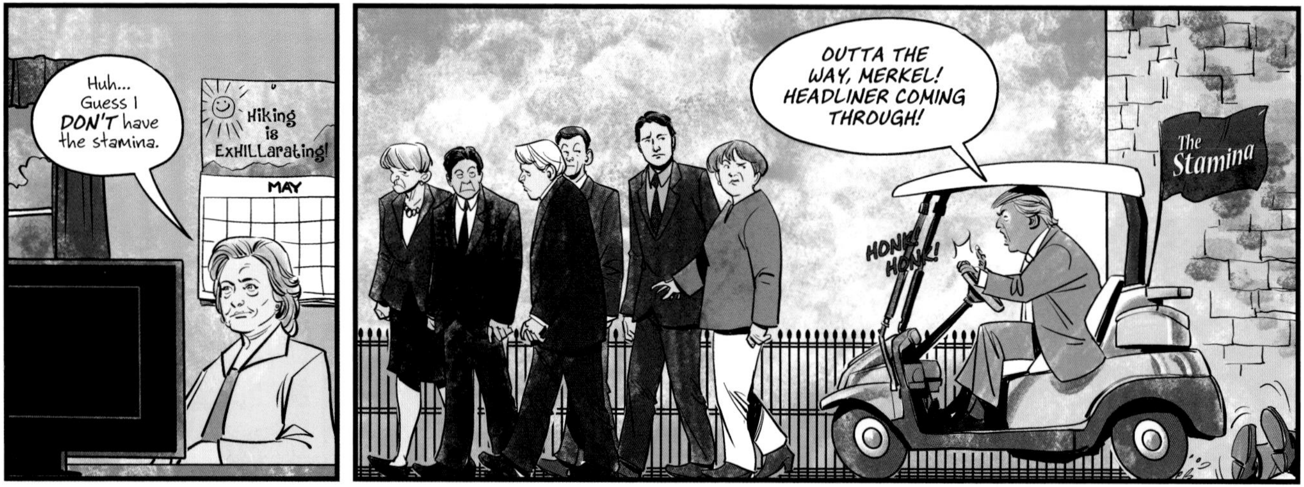

Huh... Guess I DON'T have the stamina.
Hiking is ExHILLarating!
MAY
OUTTA THE WAY, MERKEL! HEADLINER COMING THROUGH!
The Stamina
HONK! HONK!

May 31, 2017

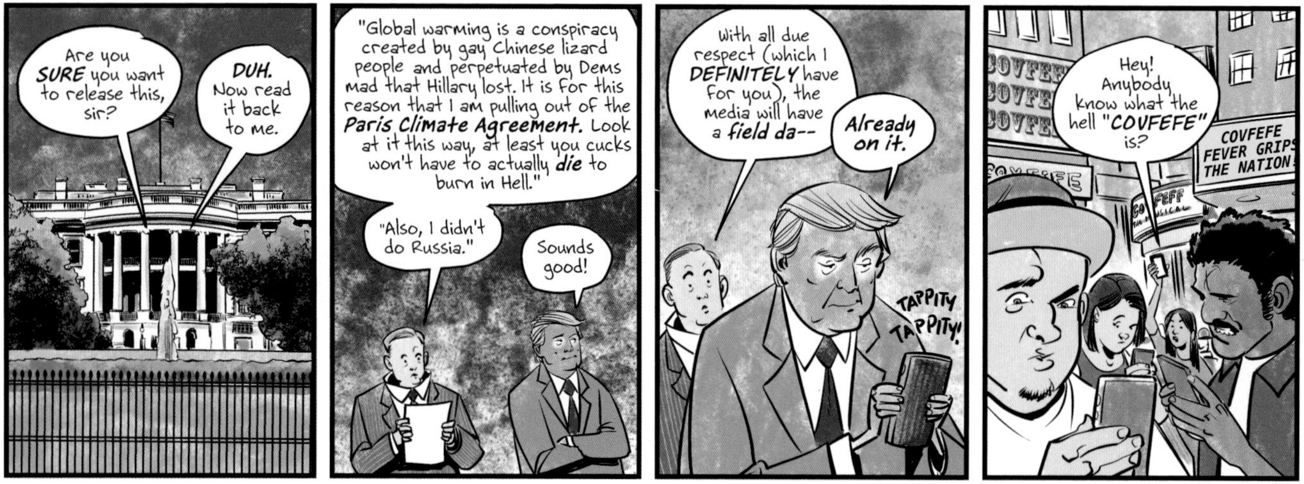

Are you SURE you want to release this, sir?
DUH. Now read it back to me.
"Global warming is a conspiracy created by gay Chinese lizard people and perpetuated by Dems mad that Hillary lost. It is for this reason that I am pulling out of the Paris Climate Agreement. Look at it this way, at least you cucks won't have to actually die to burn in Hell."
"Also, I didn't do Russia."
Sounds good!
With all due respect (which I DEFINITELY have for you), the media will have a field da--
Already on it.
TAPPITY TAPPITY!
Hey! Anybody know what the hell "COVFEFE" is?
COVFEFE FEVER GRIPS THE NATION!

Jun 2, 2017

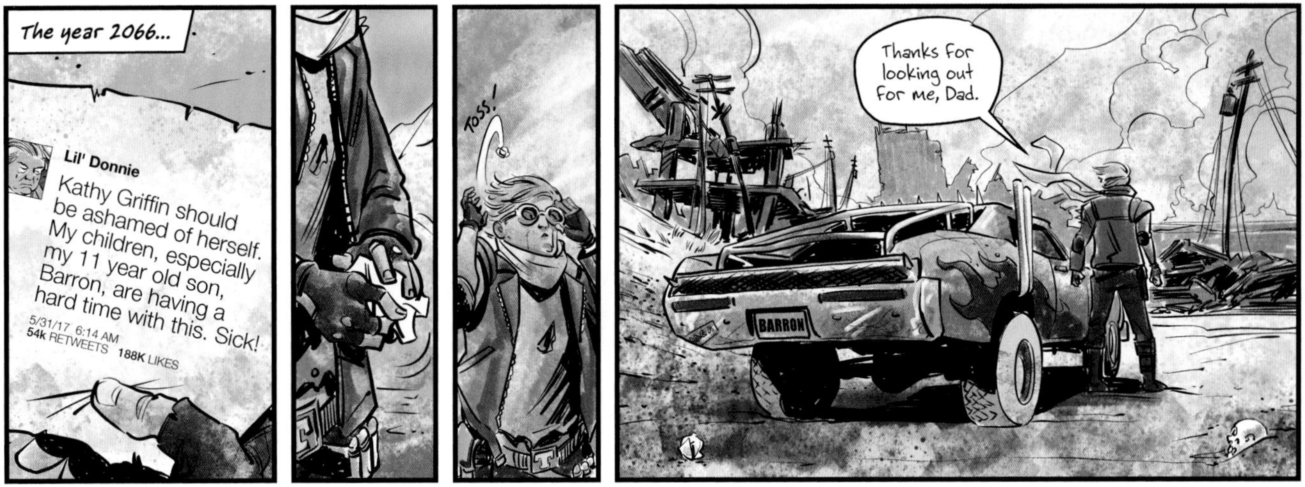
The year 2066...
Lil' Donnie
Kathy Griffin should be ashamed of herself. My children, especially my 11 year old son, Barron, are having a hard time with this. Sick!
5/31/17 6:14 AM
54k RETWEETS 188K LIKES
TOSS!
Thanks for looking out for me, Dad.
BARRON

Jun 5, 2017

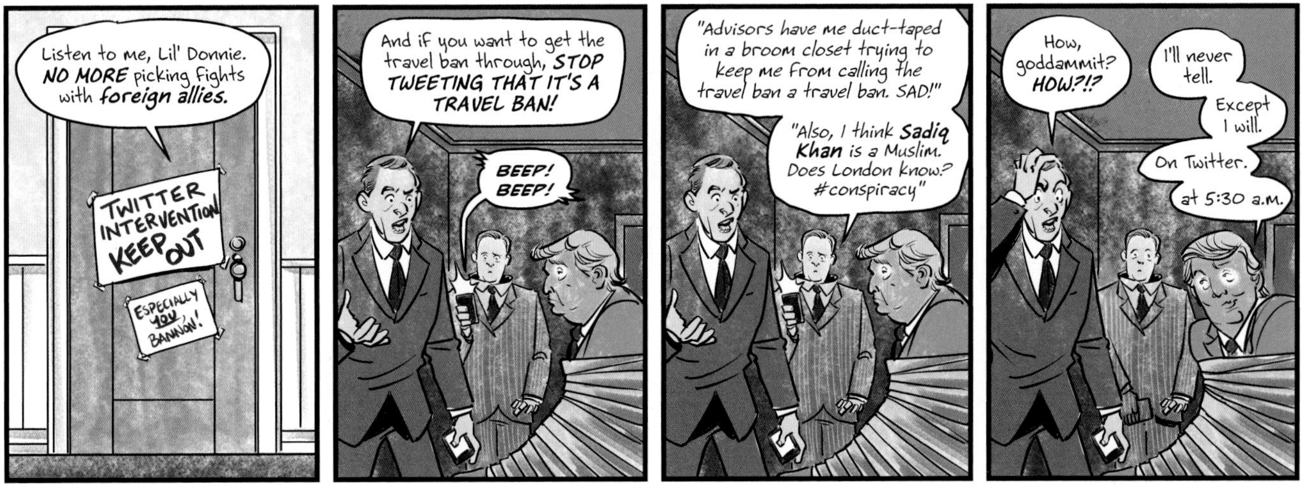
Listen to me, Lil' Donnie. NO MORE picking fights with foreign allies.
TWITTER INTERVENTION KEEP OUT
ESPECIALLY YOU, BANNON!
And if you want to get the travel ban through, STOP TWEETING THAT IT'S A TRAVEL BAN!
BEEP! BEEP!
"Advisors have me duct-taped in a broom closet trying to keep me from calling the travel ban a travel ban. SAD!"
"Also, I think Sadiq Khan is a Muslim. Does London know? #conspiracy"
How, goddammit? HOW?!?
I'll never tell.
Except I will.
On Twitter.
at 5:30 a.m.

Jun 8, 2017

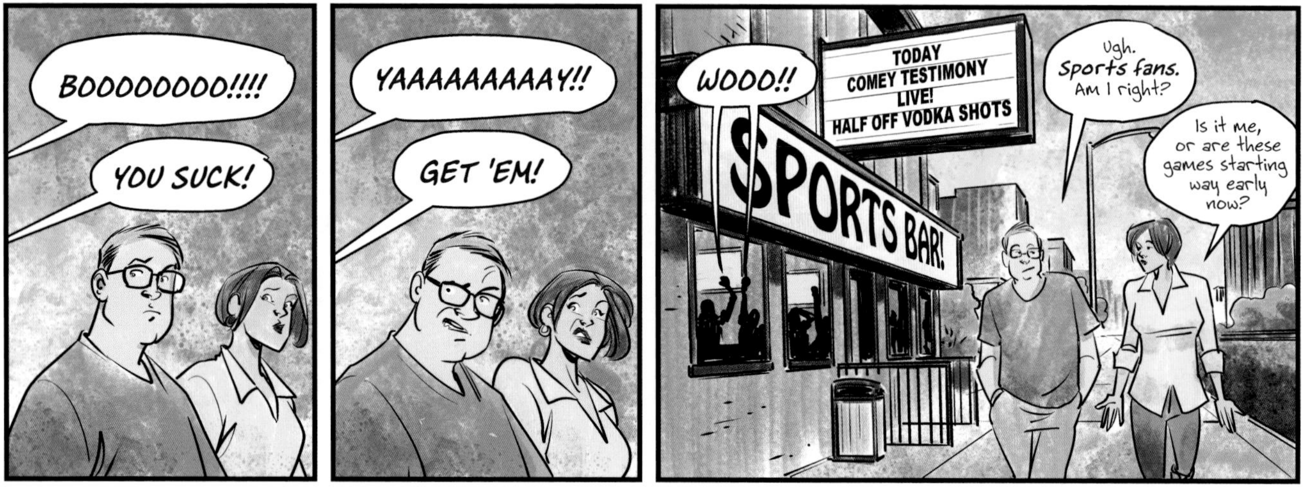
BOOOOOOOO!!!!
YOU SUCK!
YAAAAAAAAAY!!
GET 'EM!
WOOO!!
TODAY
COMEY TESTIMONY
LIVE!
HALF OFF VODKA SHOTS
SPORTS BAR!
Ugh. Sports fans. Am I right?
Is it me, or are these games starting way early now?

Jun 12, 2017

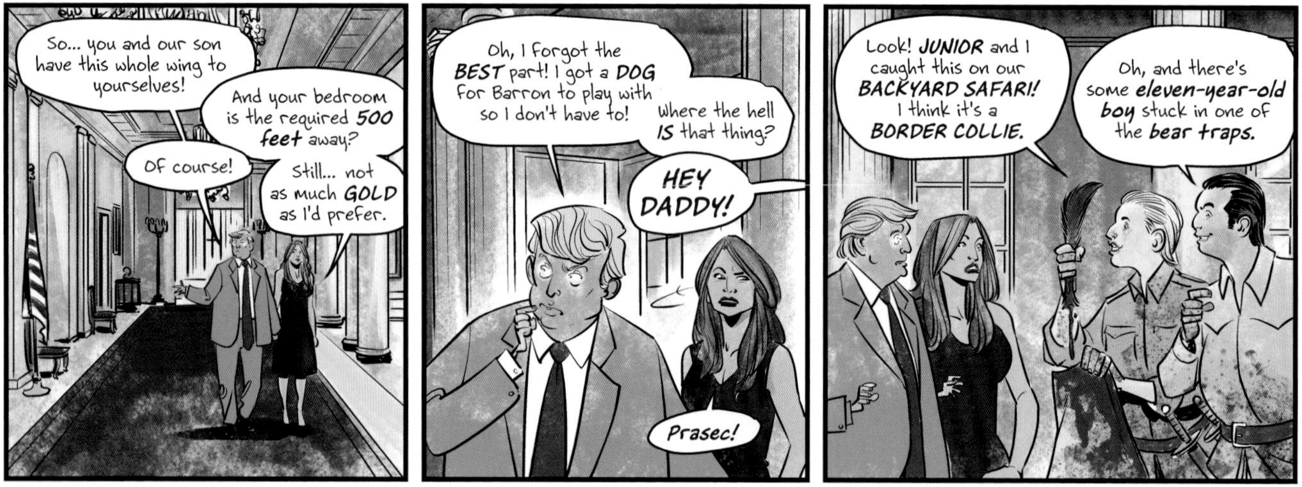
So... you and our son have this whole wing to yourselves!
And your bedroom is the required 500 feet away?
Of course!
Still... not as much GOLD as I'd prefer.
Oh, I forgot the BEST part! I got a DOG for Barron to play with so I don't have to!
Where the hell IS that thing?
HEY DADDY!
Prasec!
Look! JUNIOR and I caught this on our BACKYARD SAFARI! I think it's a BORDER COLLIE.
Oh, and there's some eleven-year-old boy stuck in one of the bear traps.

Jun 14, 2017

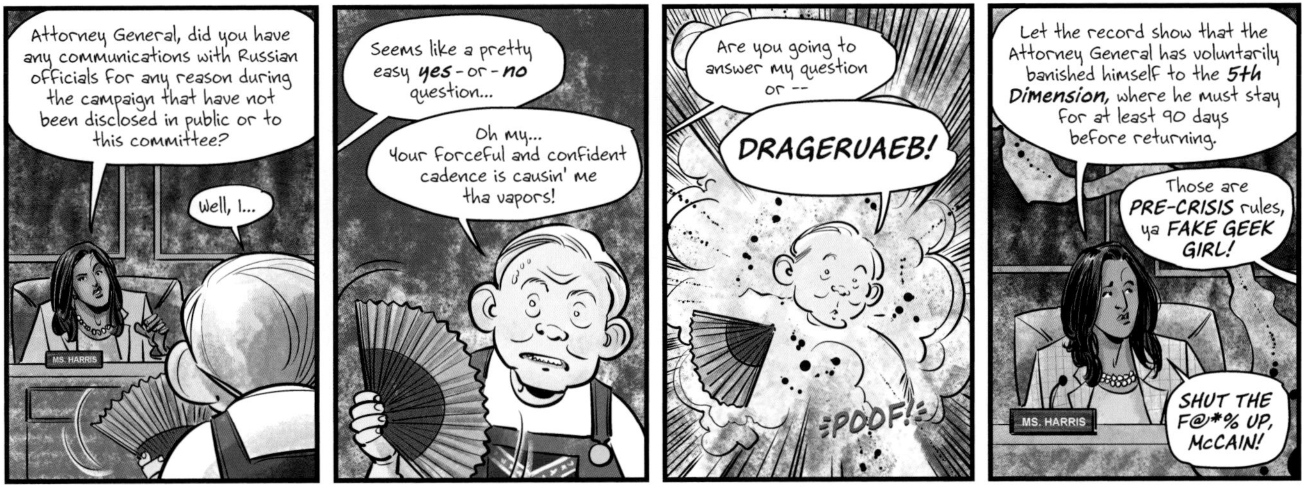
Attorney General, did you have any communications with Russian officials for any reason during the campaign that have not been disclosed in public or to this committee?
Well, I...
MS. HARRIS
Seems like a pretty easy **yes**-or-**no** question...
Oh my... Your forceful and confident cadence is causin' me tha vapors!
Are you going to answer my question or --
DRAGERUAEB!
POOF!
Let the record show that the Attorney General has voluntarily banished himself to the **5th Dimension,** where he must stay for at least 90 days before returning.
Those are **PRE-CRISIS** rules, ya **FAKE GEEK GIRL!**
MS. HARRIS
SHUT THE F@*% UP, McCAIN!

Jun 23, 2017

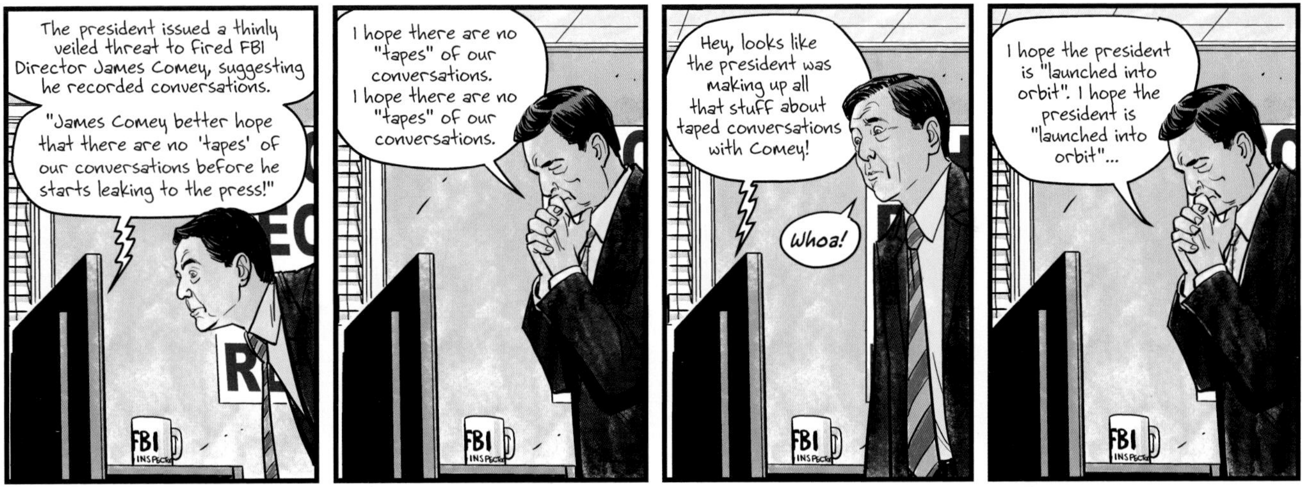
The president issued a thinly veiled threat to fired FBI Director James Comey, suggesting he recorded conversations.
"James Comey better hope that there are no 'tapes' of our conversations before he starts leaking to the press!"
FBI INSPECTOR
I hope there are no "tapes" of our conversations. I hope there are no "tapes" of our conversations.
FBI INSPECTOR
Hey, looks like the president was making up all that stuff about taped conversations with Comey!
Whoa!
FBI INSPECTOR
I hope the president is "launched into orbit". I hope the president is "launched into orbit"...
FBI INSPECTOR

Jun 26, 2017

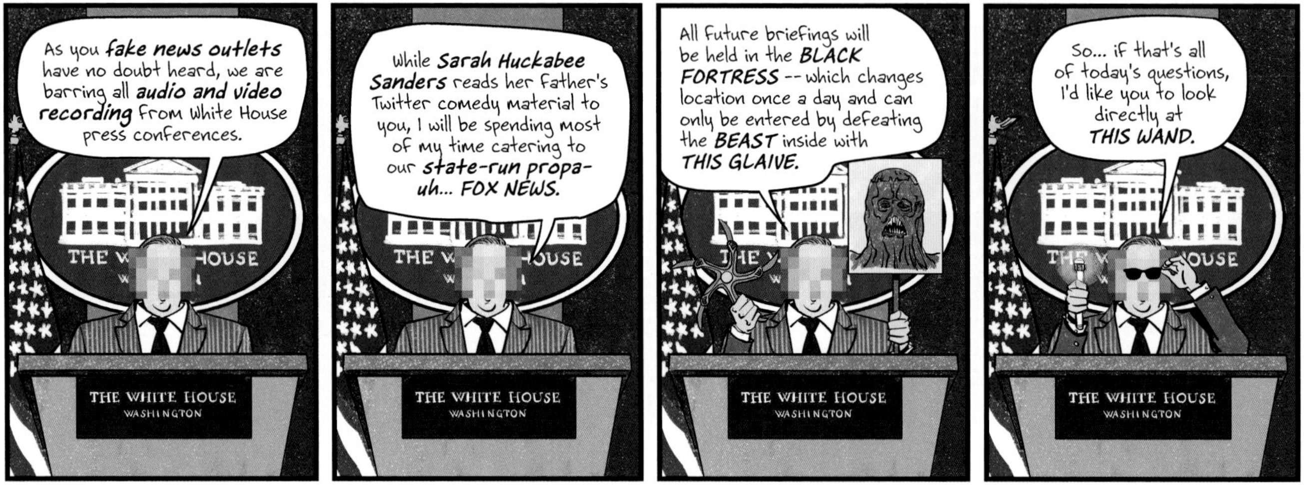
As you **fake news outlets** have no doubt heard, we are barring all **audio and video recording** from White House press conferences.
THE WHITE HOUSE WASHINGTON
While **Sarah Huckabee Sanders** reads her father's Twitter comedy material to you, I will be spending most of my time catering to our **state-run propa-** uh... **FOX NEWS.**
THE WHITE HOUSE WASHINGTON
All future briefings will be held in the **BLACK FORTRESS** -- which changes location once a day and can only be entered by defeating the **BEAST** inside with **THIS GLAIVE.**
THE WHITE HOUSE WASHINGTON
So... if that's all of today's questions, I'd like you to look directly at **THIS WAND.**
THE WHITE HOUSE WASHINGTON

Jul 1, 2017

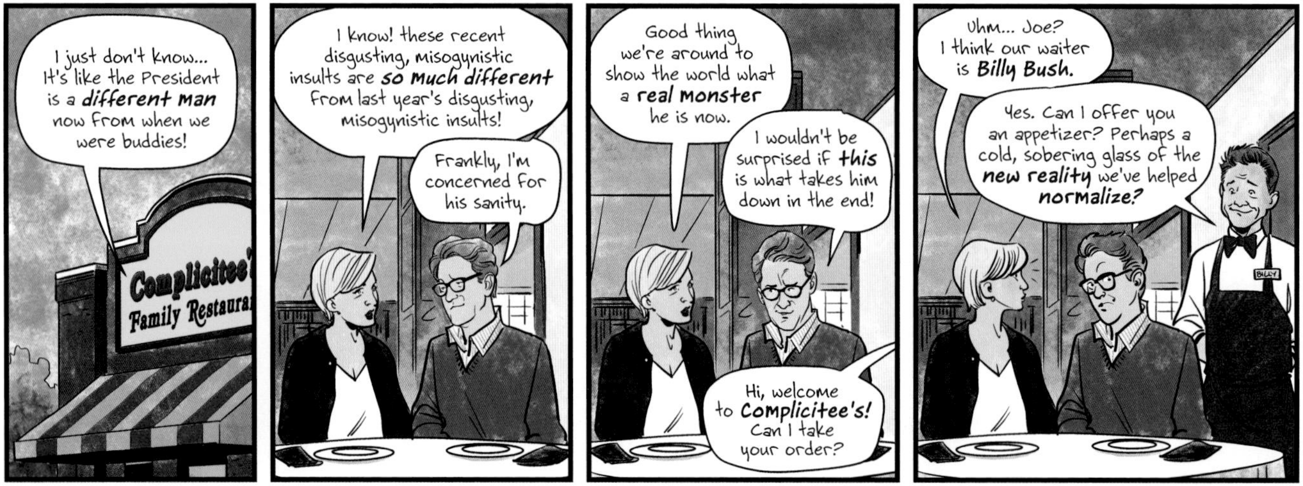
I just don't know... It's like the President is a **different man** now from when we were buddies!
Complicitee's Family Restaurant
I know! these recent disgusting, misogynistic insults are **so much different** from last year's disgusting, misogynistic insults!
Frankly, I'm concerned for his sanity.
Good thing we're around to show the world what a **real monster** he is now.
I wouldn't be surprised if **this** is what takes him down in the end!
Hi, welcome to **Complicitee's!** Can I take your order?
Uhm... Joe? I think our waiter is **Billy Bush.**
Yes. Can I offer you an appetizer? Perhaps a cold, sobering glass of the **new reality** we've helped **normalize?**
BILLY

Jul 2, 2017

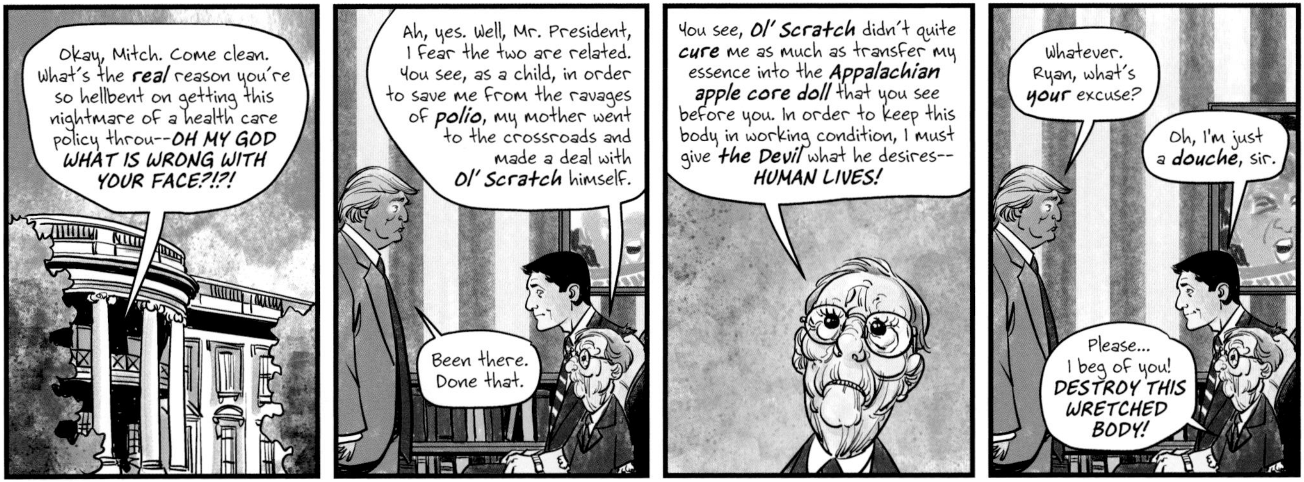
Okay, Mitch. Come clean. What's the **real** reason you're so hellbent on getting this nightmare of a health care policy throu--**OH MY GOD WHAT IS WRONG WITH YOUR FACE?!?!**
Ah, yes. Well, Mr. President, I fear the two are related. You see, as a child, in order to save me from the ravages of **polio**, my mother went to the crossroads and made a deal with **Ol' Scratch** himself.
Been there. Done that.
You see, **Ol' Scratch** didn't quite **cure** me as much as transfer my essence into the **Appalachian apple core doll** that you see before you. In order to keep this body in working condition, I must give **the Devil** what he desires--**HUMAN LIVES!**
Whatever. Ryan, what's **your** excuse?
Oh, I'm just a **douche**, sir.
Please... I beg of you! **DESTROY THIS WRETCHED BODY!**

Jul 4, 2017

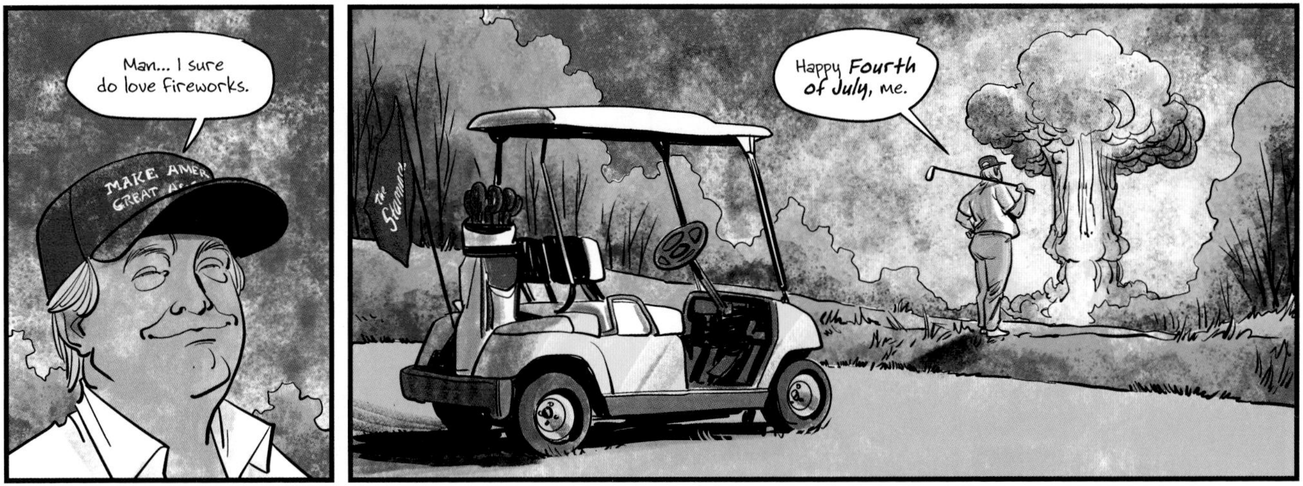
Man... I sure do love fireworks.
Happy **Fourth of July**, me.

Jul 7, 2017

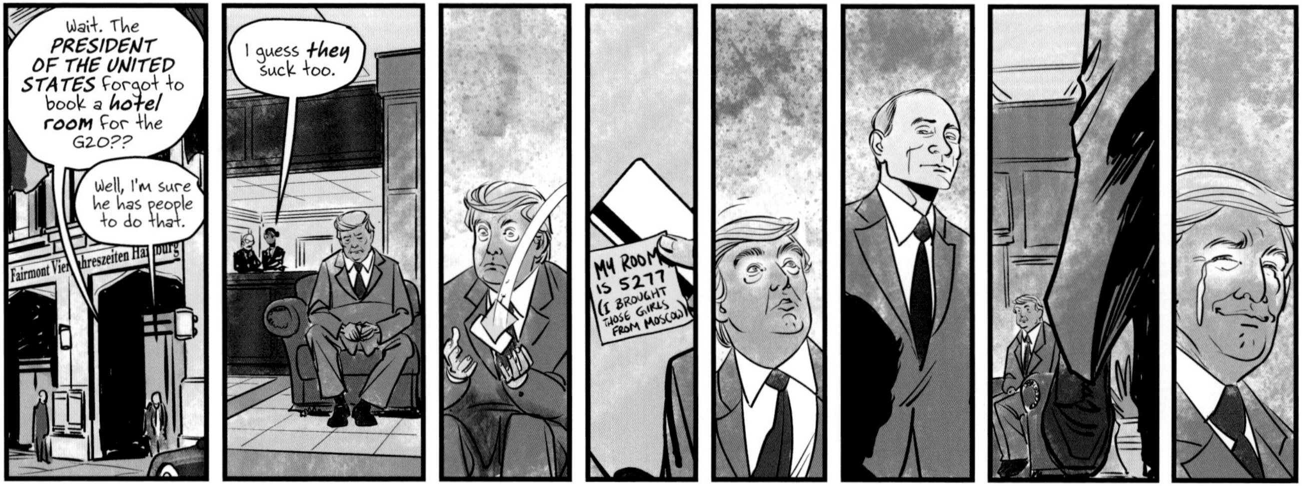
Wait. The **PRESIDENT OF THE UNITED STATES** forgot to book a ***hotel* room** for the G20??
Well, I'm sure he has people to do that.
I guess ***they*** suck too.
MY ROOM IS 5277 (I BROUGHT THOSE GIRLS FROM MOSCOW)

Jul 10, 2017

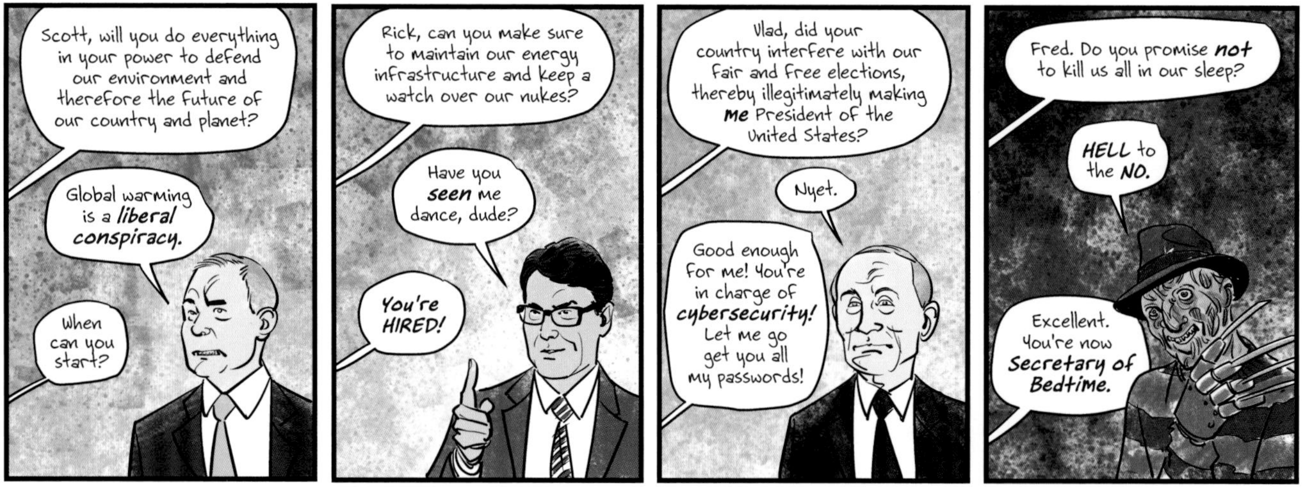
Scott, will you do everything in your power to defend our environment and therefore the future of our country and planet?
Global warming is a ***liberal* conspiracy.**
When can you start?
Rick, can you make sure to maintain our energy infrastructure and keep a watch over our nukes?
Have you ***seen*** me dance, dude?
You're HIRED!
Vlad, did your country interfere with our fair and free elections, thereby illegitimately making **me** President of the United States?
Nyet.
Good enough for me! You're in charge of ***cybersecurity!*** Let me go get you all my passwords!
Fred. Do you promise ***not*** to kill us all in our sleep?
HELL to the ***NO.***
Excellent. You're now ***Secretary of Bedtime.***

Jul 12, 2017

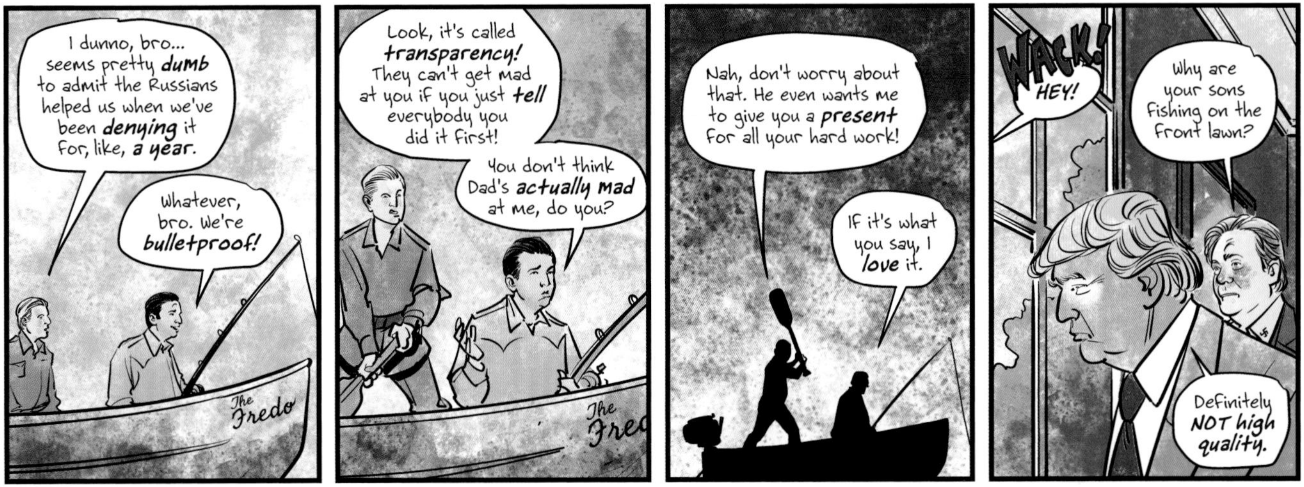
I dunno, bro... seems pretty **dumb** to admit the Russians helped us when we've been **denying** it for, like, **a year**.
Whatever, bro. We're ***bulletproof!***
The Fredo
Look, it's called ***transparency!*** They can't get mad at you if you just ***tell*** everybody you did it first!
You don't think Dad's ***actually mad*** at me, do you?
Nah, don't worry about that. He even wants me to give you a ***present*** for all your hard work!
If it's what you say, I ***love*** it.
WACK!
HEY!
Why are your sons fishing on the front lawn?
Definitely ***NOT high quality.***

Jul 17, 2017

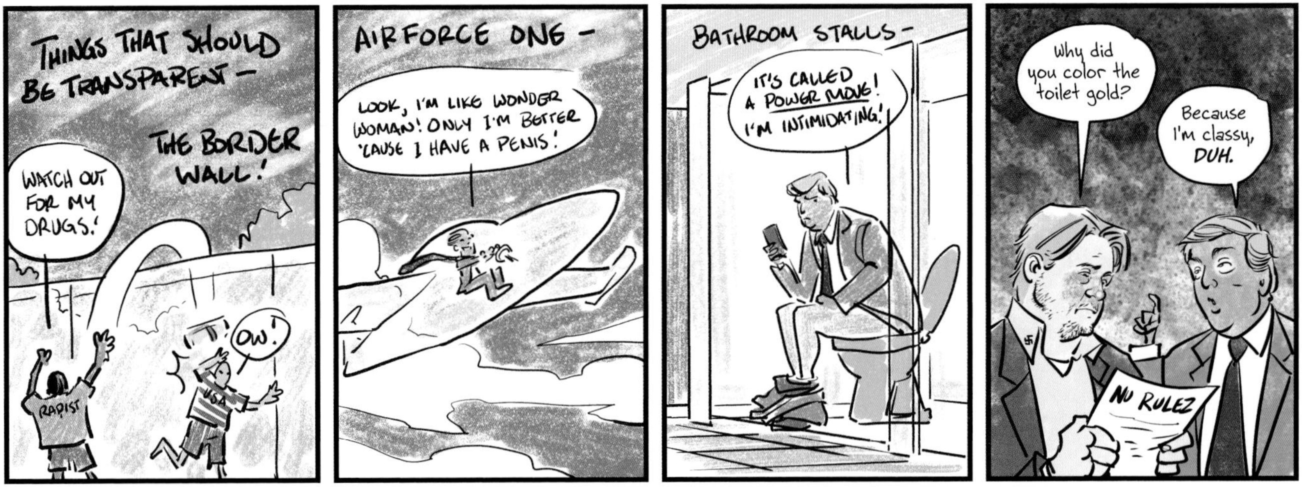
THINGS THAT SHOULD BE TRANSPARENT –
THE BORDER WALL!
WATCH OUT FOR MY DRUGS!
OW!
RAPIST
USA
AIRFORCE ONE –
LOOK, I'M LIKE WONDER WOMAN! ONLY I'M BETTER 'CAUSE I HAVE A PENIS!
BATHROOM STALLS –
IT'S CALLED A POWER MOVE! I'M INTIMIDATING!
Why did you color the toilet gold?
Because I'm classy, **DUH.**
NU RULEZ

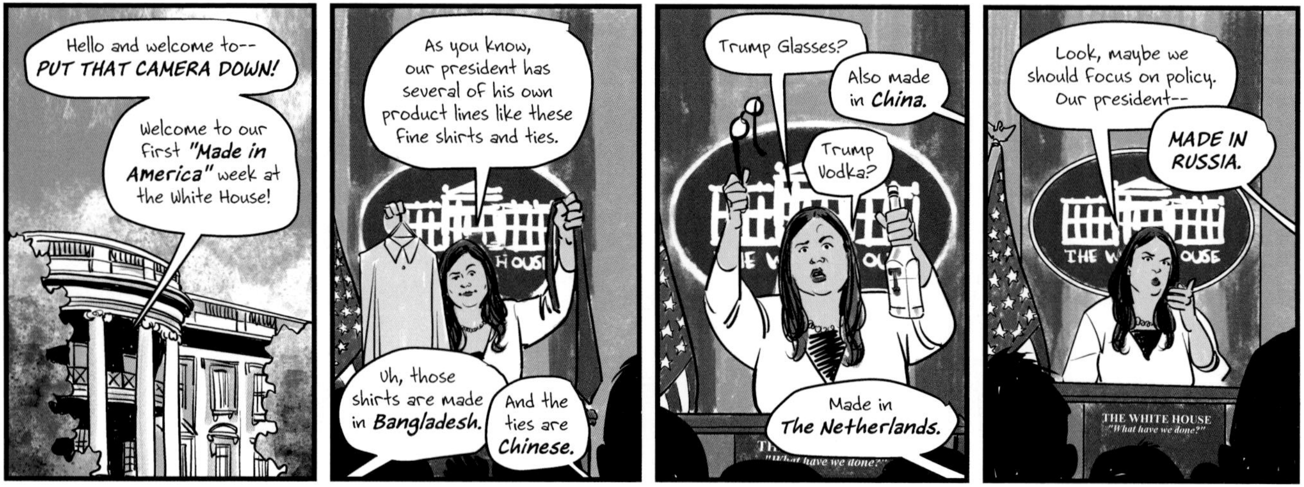
Hello and welcome to-- PUT THAT CAMERA DOWN!
Welcome to our first "Made in America" week at the White House!
As you know, our president has several of his own product lines like these fine shirts and ties.
Uh, those shirts are made in Bangladesh.
And the ties are Chinese.
Trump Glasses?
Also made in China.
Trump Vodka?
Made in The Netherlands.
Look, maybe we should focus on policy. Our president--
MADE IN RUSSIA.
THE WHITE HOUSE
"What have we done?"

Jul 19, 2017

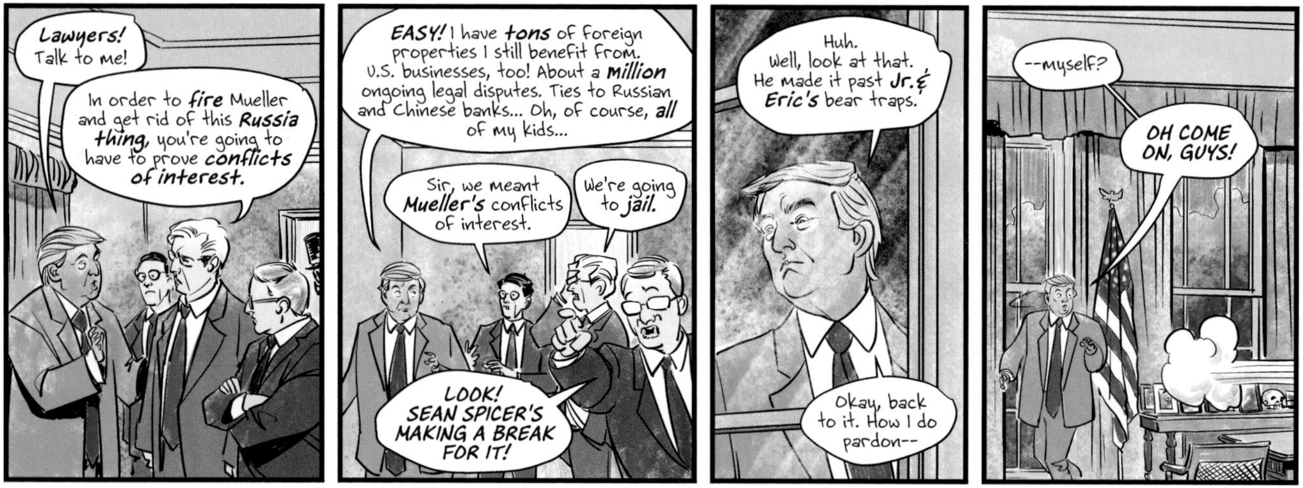
Lawyers! Talk to me!
In order to fire Mueller and get rid of this Russia thing, you're going to have to prove conflicts of interest.
EASY! I have tons of foreign properties I still benefit from. U.S. businesses, too! About a million ongoing legal disputes. Ties to Russian and Chinese banks... Oh, of course, all of my kids...
Sir, we meant Mueller's conflicts of interest.
We're going to jail.
LOOK! SEAN SPICER'S MAKING A BREAK FOR IT!
Huh. Well, look at that. He made it past Jr. & Eric's bear traps.
Okay, back to it. How I do pardon--
--myself?
OH COME ON, GUYS!

Jul 24, 2017

Jul 25, 2017

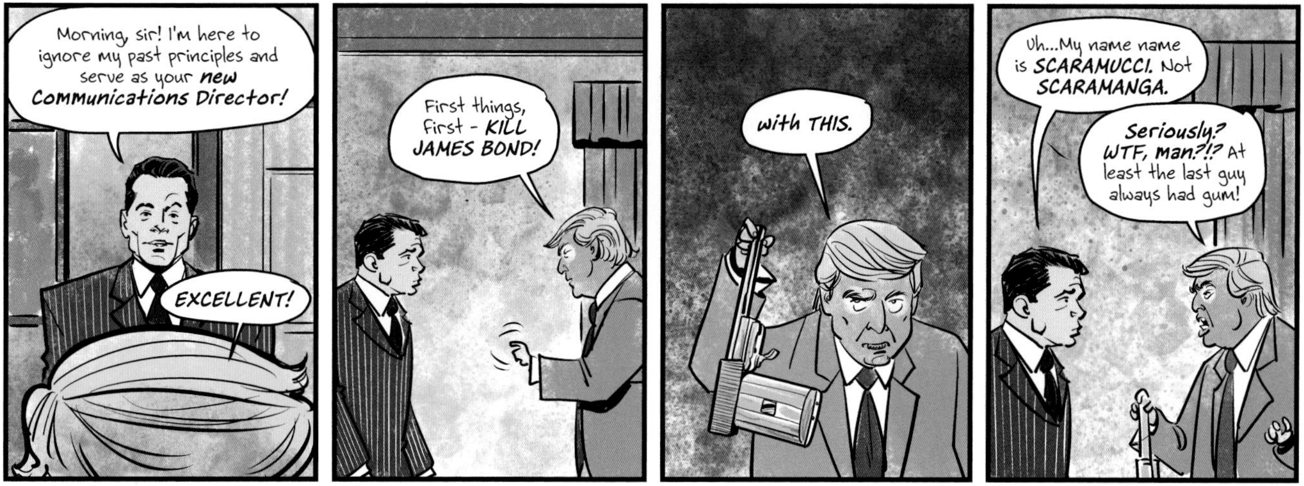

Morning, sir! I'm here to ignore my past principles and serve as your **new Communications Director!**
EXCELLENT!
First things, first - **KILL JAMES BOND!**
with THIS.
Uh...My name name is **SCARAMUCCI.** Not **SCARAMANGA.**
Seriously? WTF, man?!? At least the last guy always had gum!

Jul 26, 2017

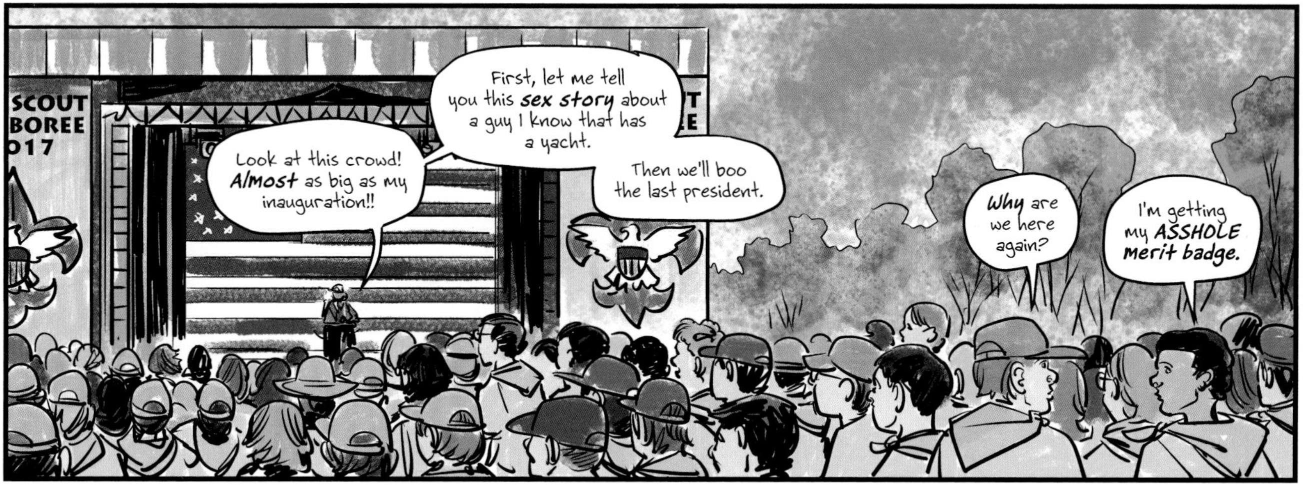

SCOUT
BOREE
017
Look at this crowd! **Almost** as big as my inauguration!!
First, let me tell you this **sex story** about a guy I know that has a yacht.
Then we'll boo the last president.
Why are we here again?
I'm getting my **ASSHOLE merit badge.**

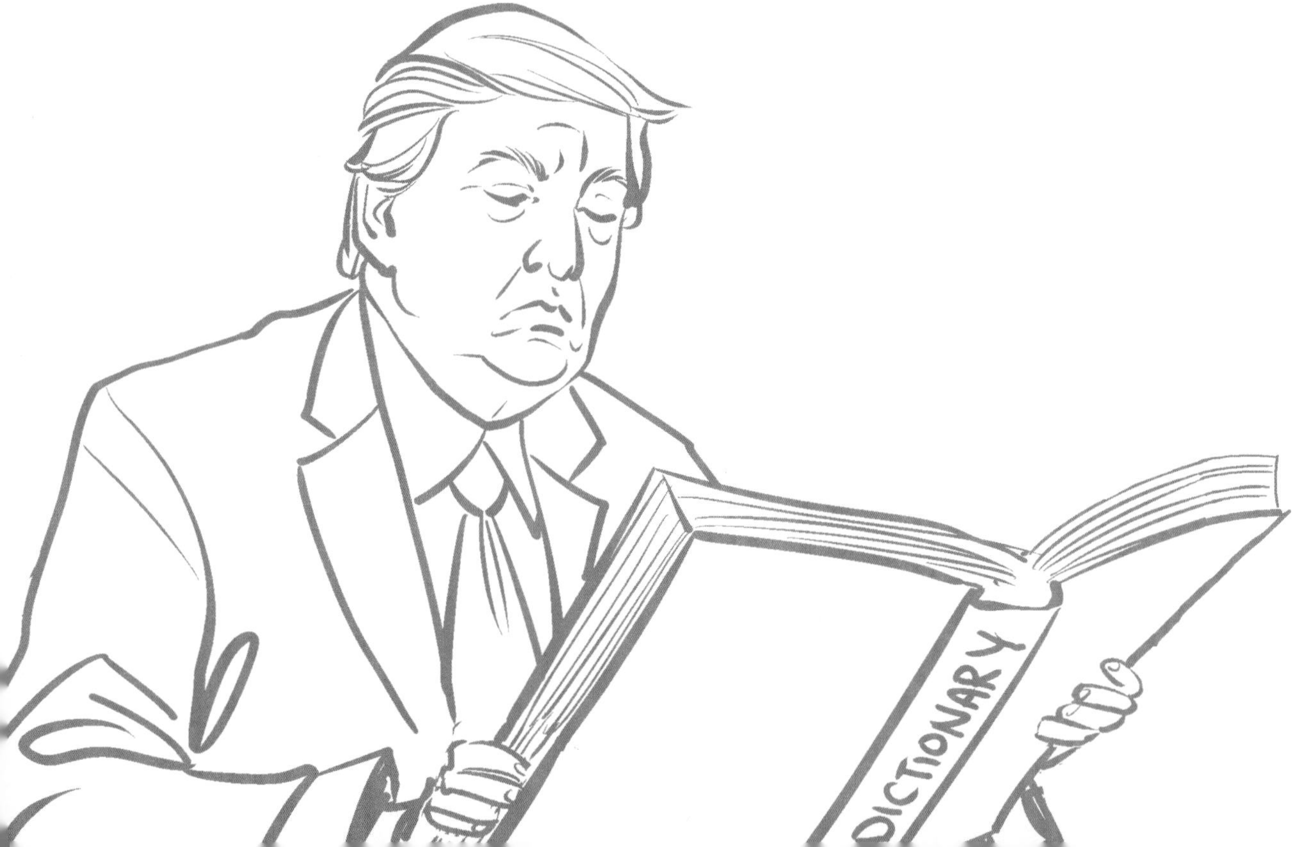
DICTIONARY

Jul 31, 2017

$12
That's what insurance costs, right?
66
JULY
THIS IS NOT A FAKE TIME MAGAZINE COVER TO HANG UP AT A GOLF CLUB. IT'S
APPROVED BY THE ACTUAL CITIZENS of AMERICA
FAKE COMIC!
LIL'
DONNIE
SLEEPY
FIRED
FLYNN
COMPLICIT
FIRED
TILLERSON
COMEY
FIRED
IVANKA
RECUSED
DRUNK
PRIEBUS
BANNON
DROPPED
SESSIONS
CHRISTIE
PENCE
RESIGNED
SPICER
2017
AFTER BYRNE

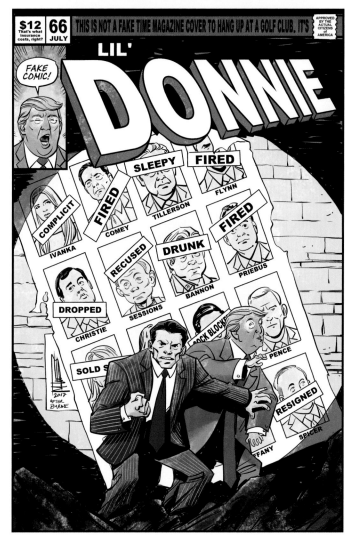

Lil' Donnie

by Mike Norton

Aug 4, 2017

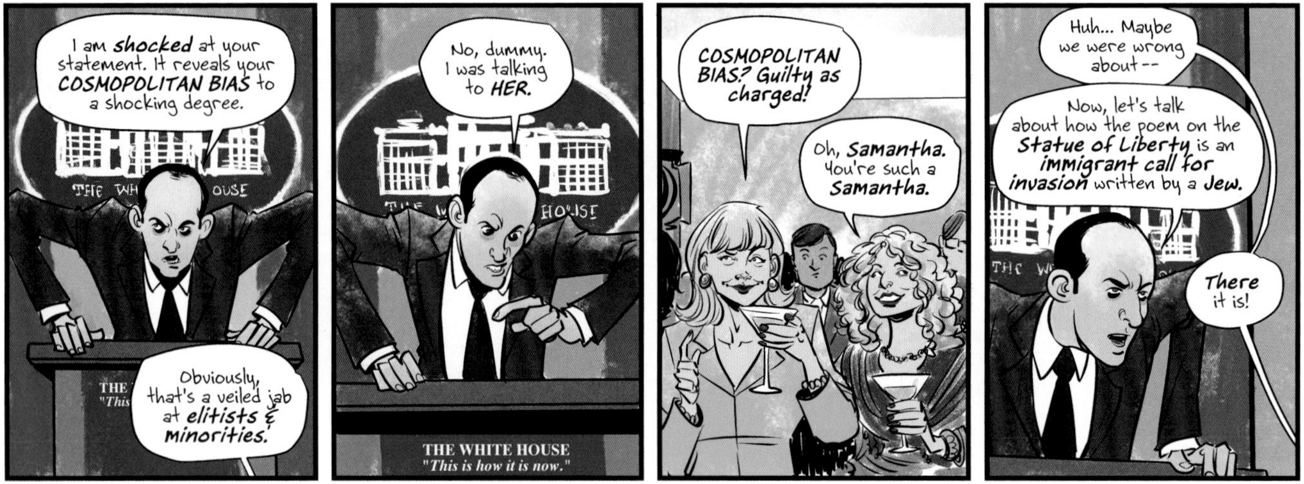
I am shocked at your statement. It reveals your COSMOPOLITAN BIAS to a shocking degree.
THE WHITE HOUSE
Obviously, that's a veiled jab at elitists & minorities.
No, dummy. I was talking to HER.
THE WHITE HOUSE
"This is how it is now."
COSMOPOLITAN BIAS? Guilty as charged!
Oh, Samantha. You're such a Samantha.
Huh... Maybe we were wrong about--
Now, let's talk about how the poem on the Statue of Liberty is an immigrant call for invasion written by a Jew.
There it is!

lildonniecomic.com

Aug 7, 2017

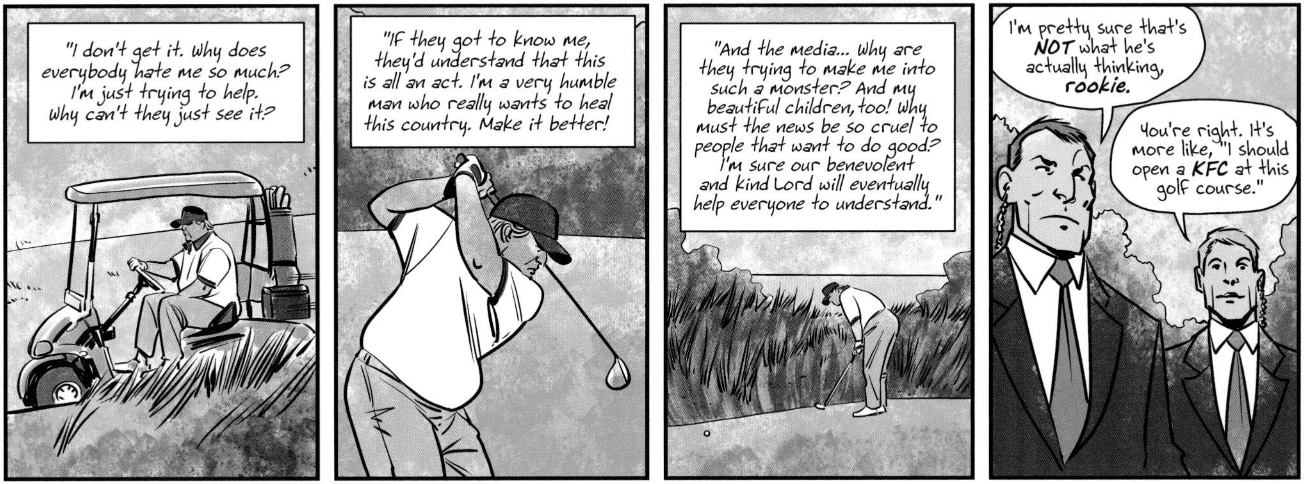
"I don't get it. Why does everybody hate me so much? I'm just trying to help. Why can't they just see it?
"If they got to know me, they'd understand that this is all an act. I'm a very humble man who really wants to heal this country. Make it better!
"And the media... Why are they trying to make me into such a monster? And my beautiful children, too! Why must the news be so cruel to people that want to do good? I'm sure our benevolent and kind Lord will eventually help everyone to understand."
I'm pretty sure that's NOT what he's actually thinking, rookie.
You're right. It's more like, "I should open a KFC at this golf course."

Aug 9, 2017

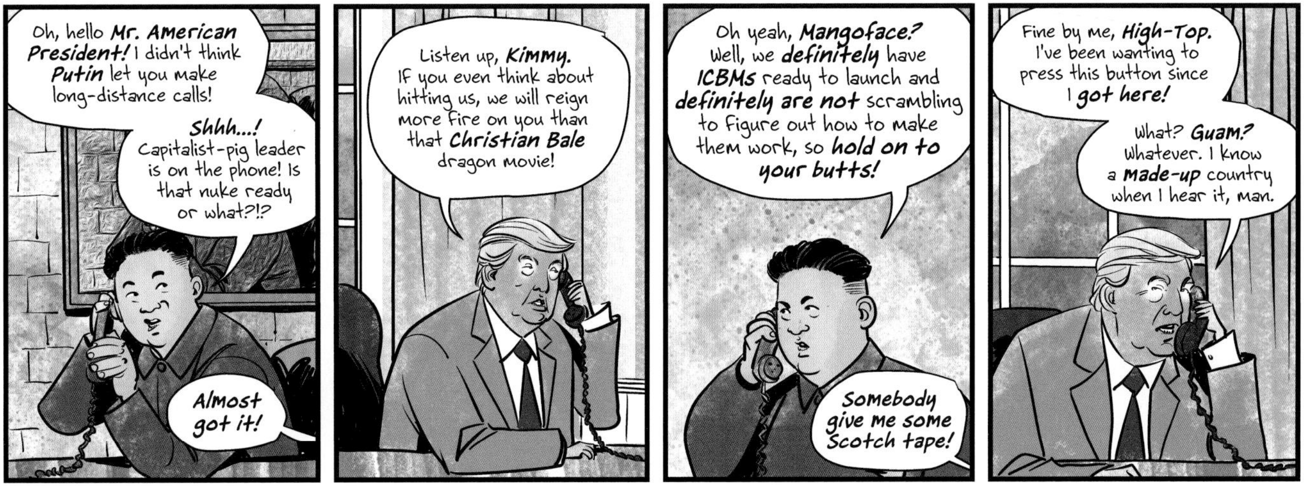
Oh, hello Mr. American President! I didn't think Putin let you make long-distance calls!
Shhh...! Capitalist-pig leader is on the phone! Is that nuke ready or what?!?
Almost got it!
Listen up, Kimmy. If you even think about hitting us, we will reign more fire on you than that Christian Bale dragon movie!
Oh yeah, Mangoface? Well, we definitely have ICBMs ready to launch and definitely are not scrambling to figure out how to make them work, so hold on to your butts!
Somebody give me some Scotch tape!
Fine by me, High-Top. I've been wanting to press this button since I got here!
What? Guam? Whatever. I know a made-up country when I hear it, man.

Aug 15, 2017

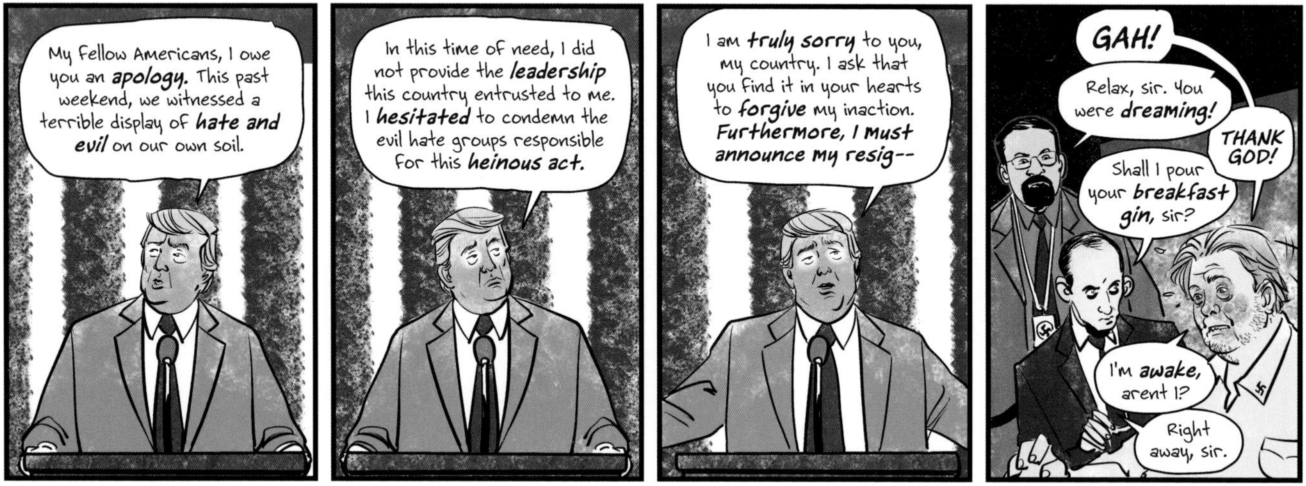
My Fellow Americans, I owe you an apology. This past weekend, we witnessed a terrible display of hate and evil on our own soil.
In this time of need, I did not provide the leadership this country entrusted to me. I hesitated to condemn the evil hate groups responsible for this heinous act.
I am truly sorry to you, my country. I ask that you find it in your hearts to forgive my inaction. Furthermore, I must announce my resig--
GAH!
Relax, sir. You were dreaming!
THANK GOD!
Shall I pour your breakfast gin, sir?
I'm awake, arent I?
Right away, sir.

Aug 18, 2017

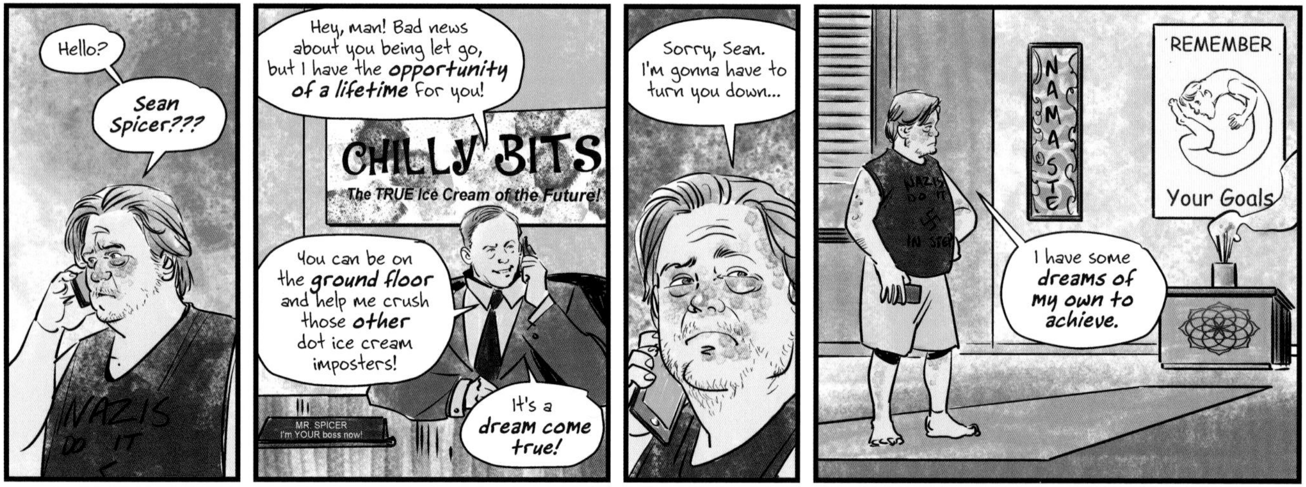
Hello?
Sean Spicer???
NAZIS
DO IT
Hey, man! Bad news about you being let go, but I have the opportunity of a lifetime for you!
CHILLY BITS
The TRUE Ice Cream of the Future!
You can be on the ground floor and help me crush those other dot ice cream imposters!
MR. SPICER
I'm YOUR boss now!
It's a dream come true!
Sorry, Sean. I'm gonna have to turn you down...
NAMASTE
REMEMBER
Your Goals
I have some dreams of my own to achieve.

Aug 22, 2017

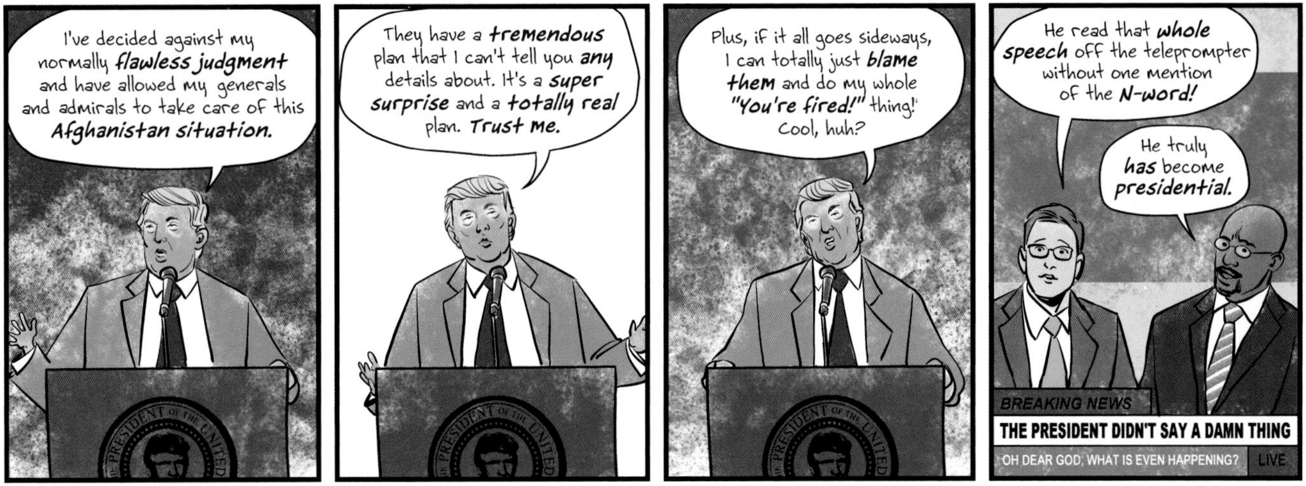

I've decided against my normally flawless judgment and have allowed my generals and admirals to take care of this Afghanistan situation.
They have a tremendous plan that I can't tell you any details about. It's a super surprise and a totally real plan. Trust me.
Plus, if it all goes sideways, I can totally just blame them and do my whole "You're fired!" thing! Cool, huh?
He read that whole speech off the teleprompter without one mention of the N-word!
He truly has become presidential.
BREAKING NEWS
THE PRESIDENT DIDN'T SAY A DAMN THING
OH DEAR GOD, WHAT IS EVEN HAPPENING?
LIVE

Sep 14, 2017

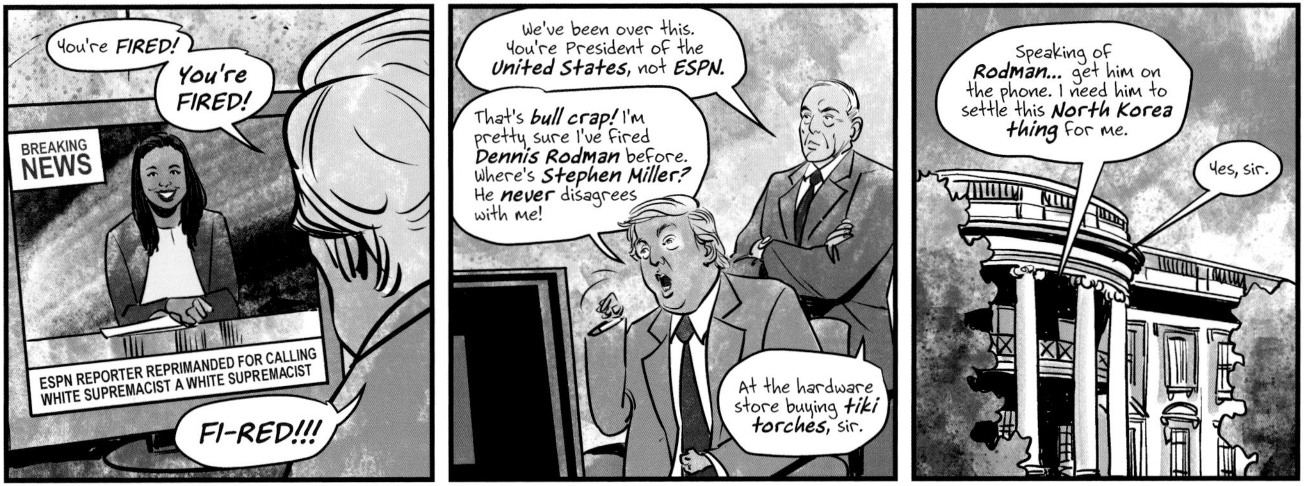

You're FIRED!
You're FIRED!
BREAKING NEWS
ESPN REPORTER REPRIMANDED FOR CALLING WHITE SUPREMACIST A WHITE SUPREMACIST
FI-RED!!!
We've been over this. You're President of the United States, not ESPN.
That's bull crap! I'm pretty sure I've fired Dennis Rodman before. Where's Stephen Miller? He never disagrees with me!
At the hardware store buying tiki torches, sir.
Speaking of Rodman... get him on the phone. I need him to settle this North Korea thing for me.
Yes, sir.

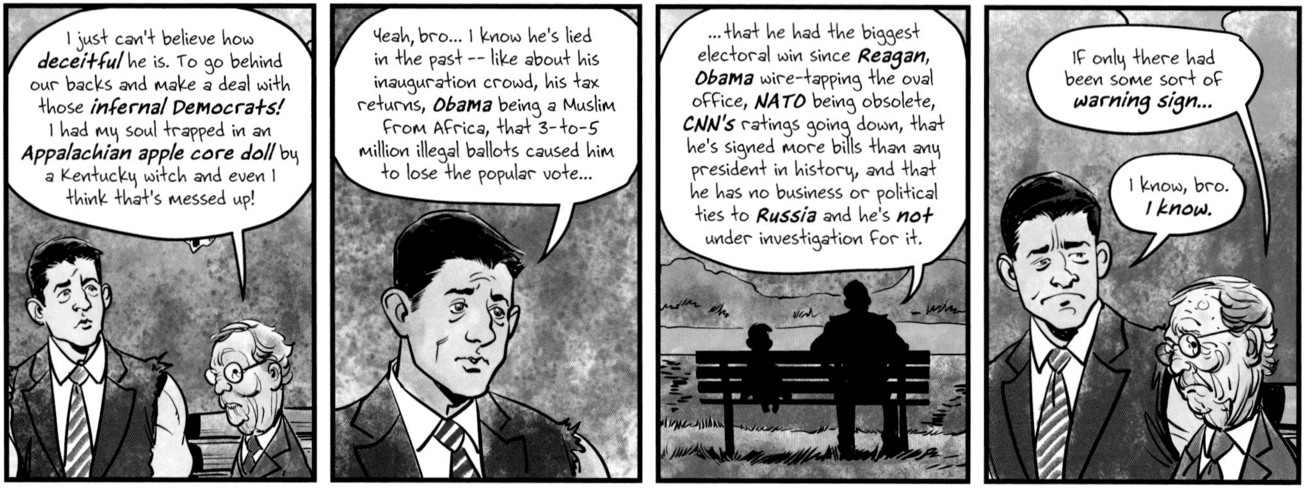
I just can't believe how **deceitful** he is. To go behind our backs and make a deal with those **infernal Democrats!** I had my soul trapped in an **Appalachian apple core doll** by a Kentucky witch and even I think that's messed up!
Yeah, bro... I know he's lied in the past -- like about his inauguration crowd, his tax returns, **Obama** being a Muslim from Africa, that 3-to-5 million illegal ballots caused him to lose the popular vote...
...that he had the biggest electoral win since **Reagan**, **Obama** wire-tapping the oval office, **NATO** being obsolete, **CNN's** ratings going down, that he's signed more bills than any president in history, and that he has no business or political ties to **Russia** and he's **not** under investigation for it.
If only there had been some sort of **warning sign...**
I know, bro. **I know.**

Sep 18, 2017

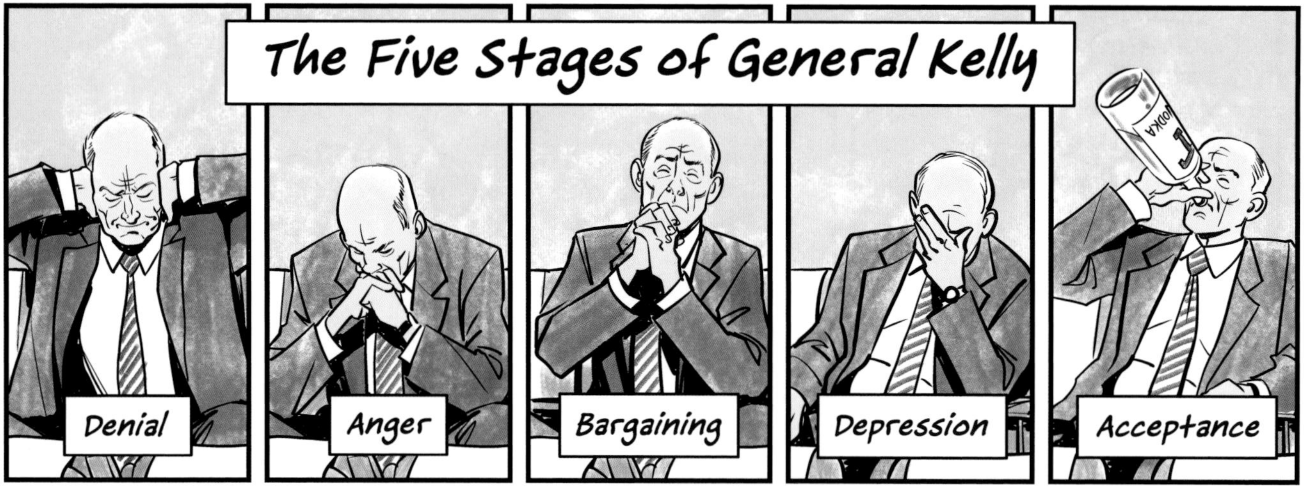
The Five Stages of General Kelly
Denial
Anger
Bargaining
Depression
Acceptance

Sep 20, 2017

Sep 22, 2017

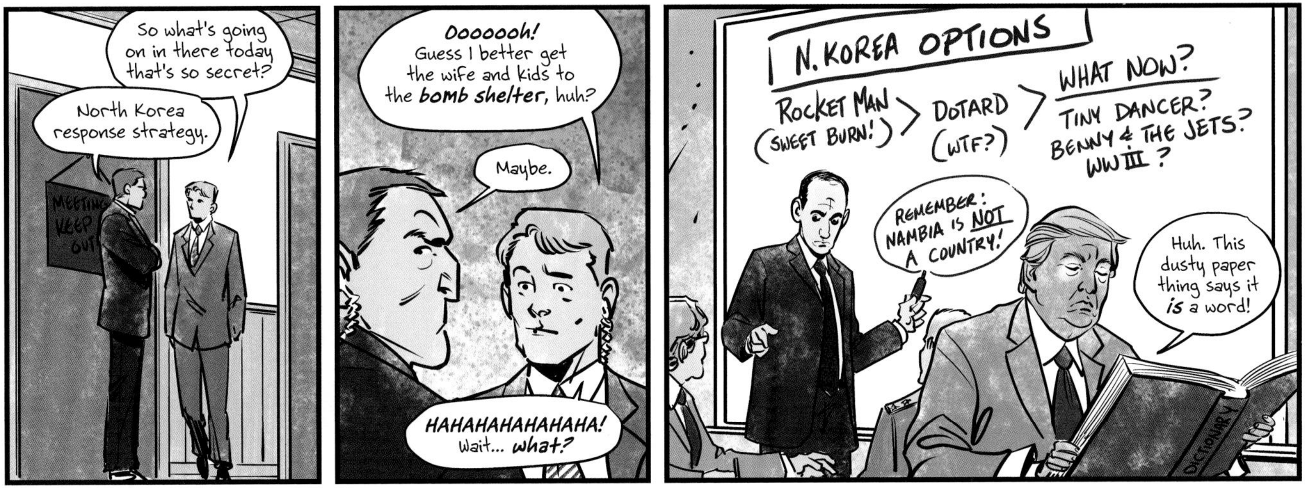
So what's going on in there today that's so secret?
North Korea response strategy.
Ooooooh! Guess I better get the wife and kids to the bomb shelter, huh?
Maybe.
HAHAHAHAHAHAHA! Wait... what?
N. KOREA OPTIONS
ROCKET MAN (SWEET BURN!) > DOTARD (WTF?) > WHAT NOW?
TINY DANCER? BENNY & THE JETS? WW III ?
REMEMBER: NAMBIA IS NOT A COUNTRY!
Huh. This dusty paper thing says it is a word!
DICTIONARY

Sep 25, 2017

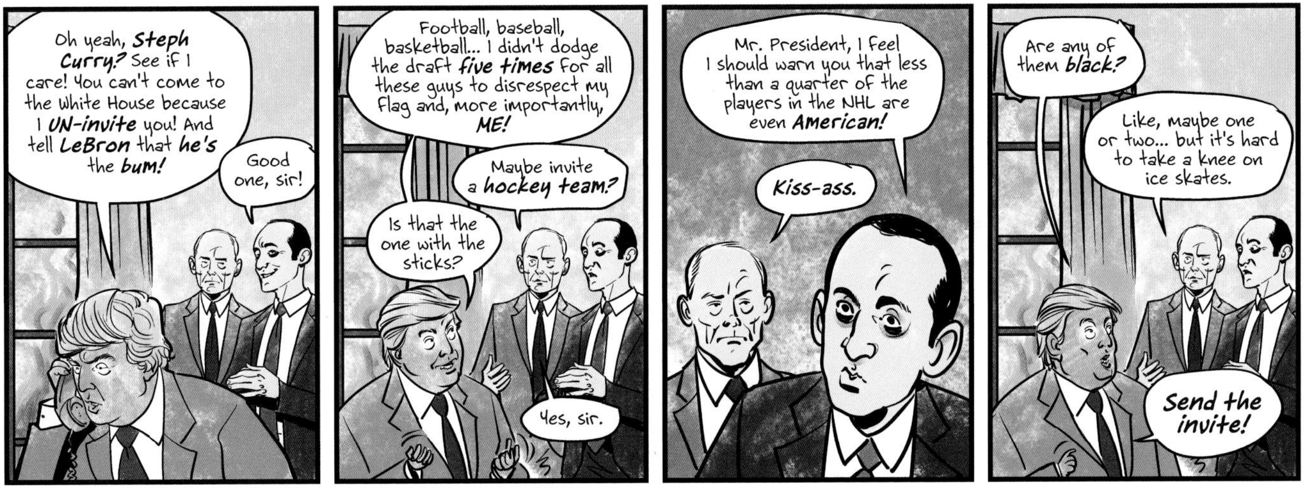
Oh yeah, Steph Curry? See if I care! You can't come to the White House because I UN-invite you! And tell LeBron that he's the bum!
Good one, sir!
Football, baseball, basketball... I didn't dodge the draft five times for all these guys to disrespect my flag and, more importantly, ME!
Maybe invite a hockey team?
Is that the one with the sticks?
Yes, sir.
Mr. President, I feel I should warn you that less than a quarter of the players in the NHL are even American!
Kiss-ass.
Are any of them black?
Like, maybe one or two... but it's hard to take a knee on ice skates.
Send the invite!

Sep 27, 2017

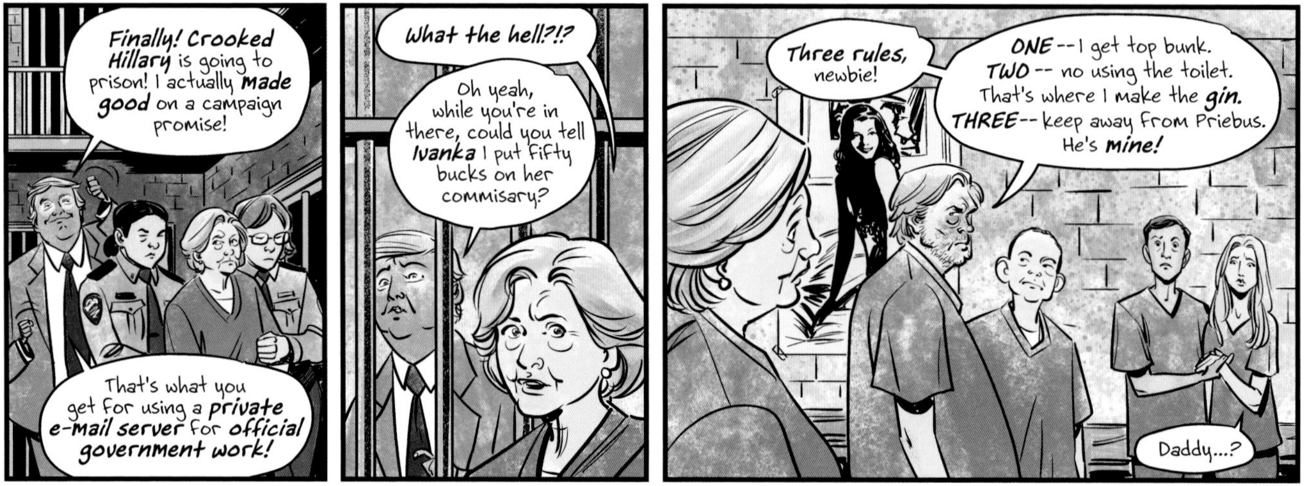
Finally! Crooked Hillary is going to prison! I actually made good on a campaign promise!
That's what you get for using a private e-mail server for official government work!
What the hell?!?
Oh yeah, while you're in there, could you tell Ivanka I put fifty bucks on her commisary?
Three rules, newbie!
ONE--I get top bunk. TWO-- no using the toilet. That's where I make the gin. THREE-- keep away from Priebus. He's mine!
Daddy...?

Sep 30, 2017

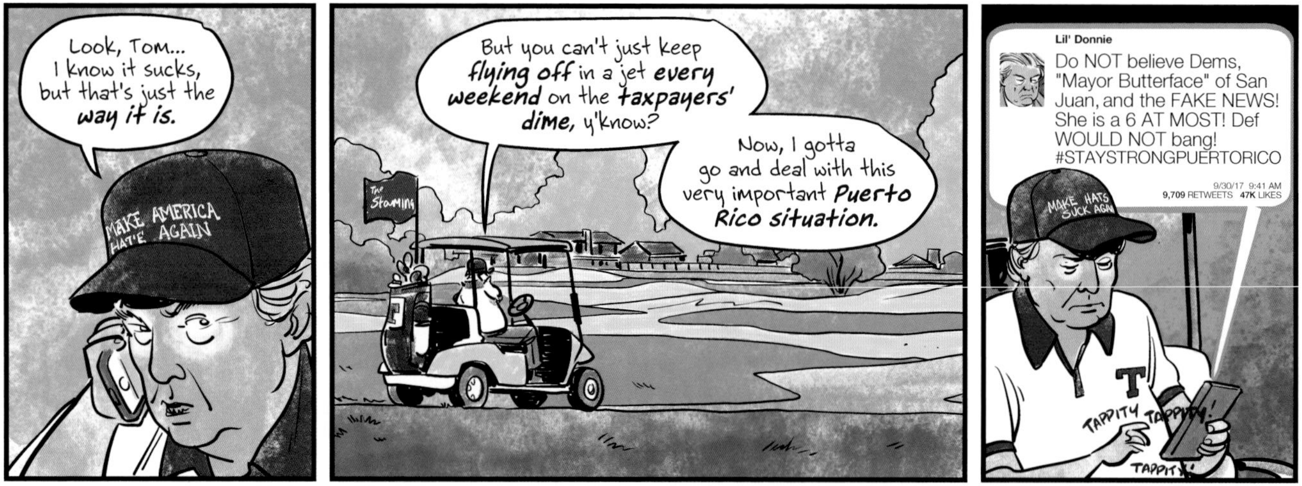
Look, Tom... I know it sucks, but that's just the way it is.
MAKE AMERICA HATE AGAIN
But you can't just keep flying off in a jet every weekend on the taxpayers' dime, y'know?
Now, I gotta go and deal with this very important Puerto Rico situation.
Lil' Donnie
Do NOT believe Dems, "Mayor Butterface" of San Juan, and the FAKE NEWS! She is a 6 AT MOST! Def WOULD NOT bang! #STAYSTRONGPUERTORICO
9/30/17 9:41 AM
9,709 RETWEETS 47K LIKES
MAKE HATS SUCK AGAIN
TAPPITY TAPPITY!
TAPPITY!

Oct 3, 2017

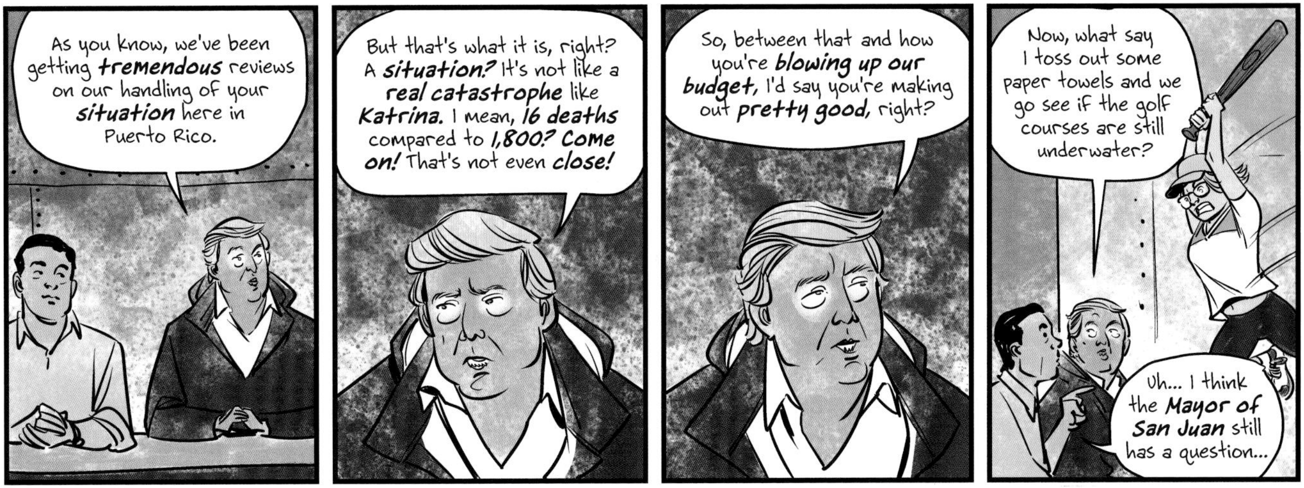
As you know, we've been getting **tremendous** reviews on our handling of your **situation** here in Puerto Rico.
But that's what it is, right? A **situation?** It's not like a **real catastrophe** like **Katrina.** I mean, **16 deaths** compared to **1,800? Come on!** That's not even **close!**
So, between that and how you're **blowing up our budget,** I'd say you're making out **pretty good,** right?
Now, what say I toss out some paper towels and we go see if the golf courses are still underwater?
Uh... I think the **Mayor of San Juan** still has a question...

Oct 5, 2017

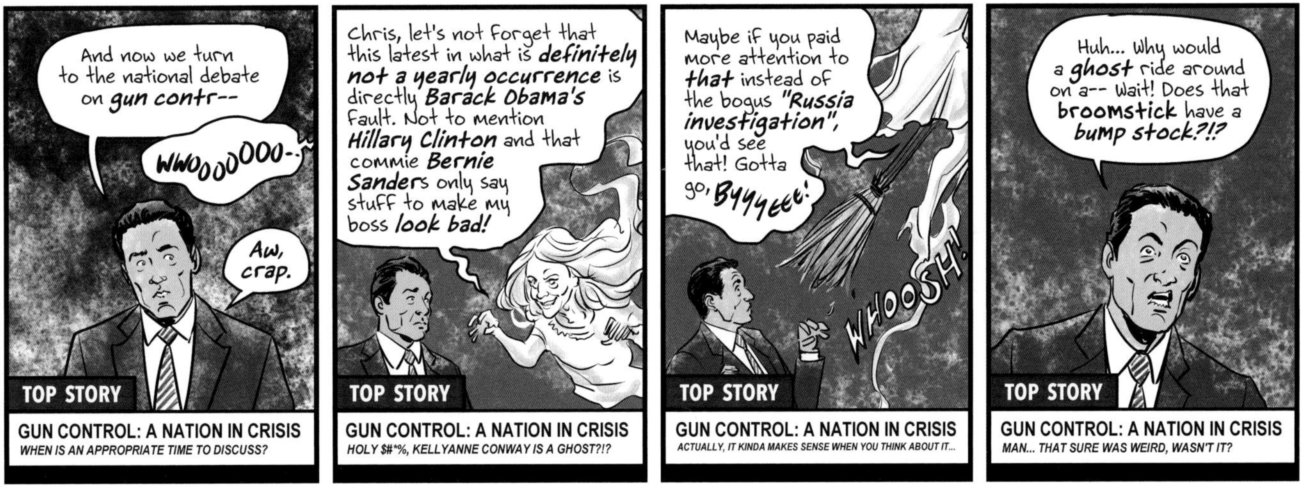
And now we turn to the national debate on **gun contr--**
WWOOOOOOO--
Aw, crap.
TOP STORY
GUN CONTROL: A NATION IN CRISIS
WHEN IS AN APPROPRIATE TIME TO DISCUSS?
Chris, let's not forget that this latest in what is **definitely not a yearly occurrence** is directly **Barack Obama's** fault. Not to mention **Hillary Clinton** and that commie **Bernie Sanders** only say stuff to make my boss **look bad!**
TOP STORY
GUN CONTROL: A NATION IN CRISIS
HOLY $#*%, KELLYANNE CONWAY IS A GHOST?!?
Maybe if you paid more attention to **that** instead of the bogus **"Russia investigation"**, you'd see that! Gotta go, Byyyeee!
WHOOSH!
TOP STORY
GUN CONTROL: A NATION IN CRISIS
ACTUALLY, IT KINDA MAKES SENSE WHEN YOU THINK ABOUT IT...
Huh... Why would a **ghost** ride around on a-- Wait! Does that **broomstick** have a **bump stock?!?**
TOP STORY
GUN CONTROL: A NATION IN CRISIS
MAN... THAT SURE WAS WEIRD, WASN'T IT?

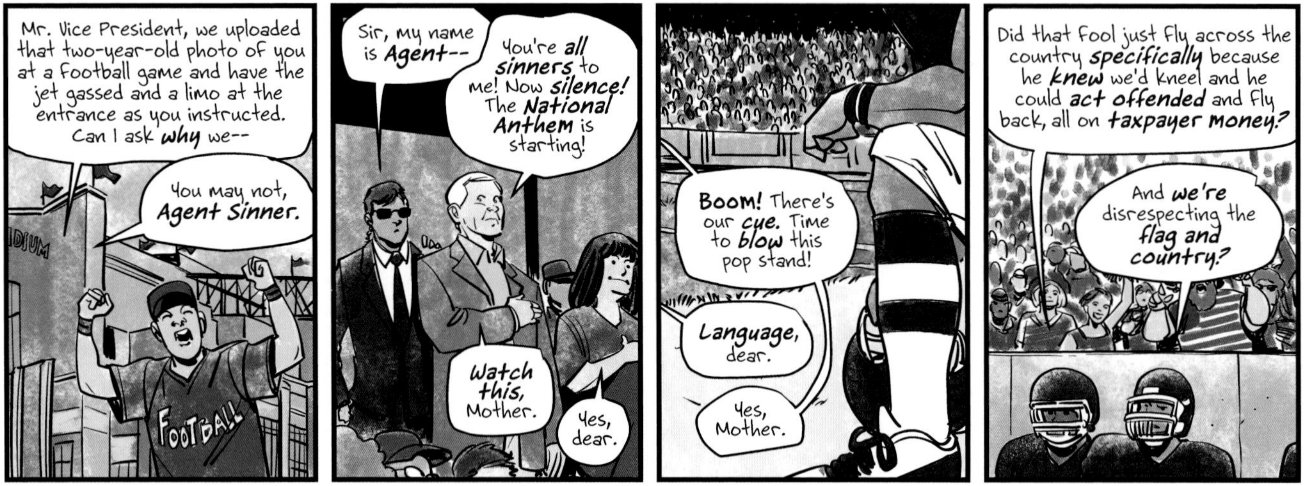
Mr. Vice President, we uploaded that two-year-old photo of you at a football game and have the jet gassed and a limo at the entrance as you instructed. Can I ask why we--
You may not, Agent Sinner.
FOOTBALL
Sir, my name is Agent--
You're all sinners to me! Now silence! The National Anthem is starting!
Watch this, Mother.
Yes, dear.
Boom! There's our cue. Time to blow this pop stand!
Language, dear.
Yes, Mother.
Did that fool just fly across the country specifically because he knew we'd kneel and he could act offended and fly back, all on taxpayer money?
And we're disrespecting the flag and country?

Oct 9, 2017

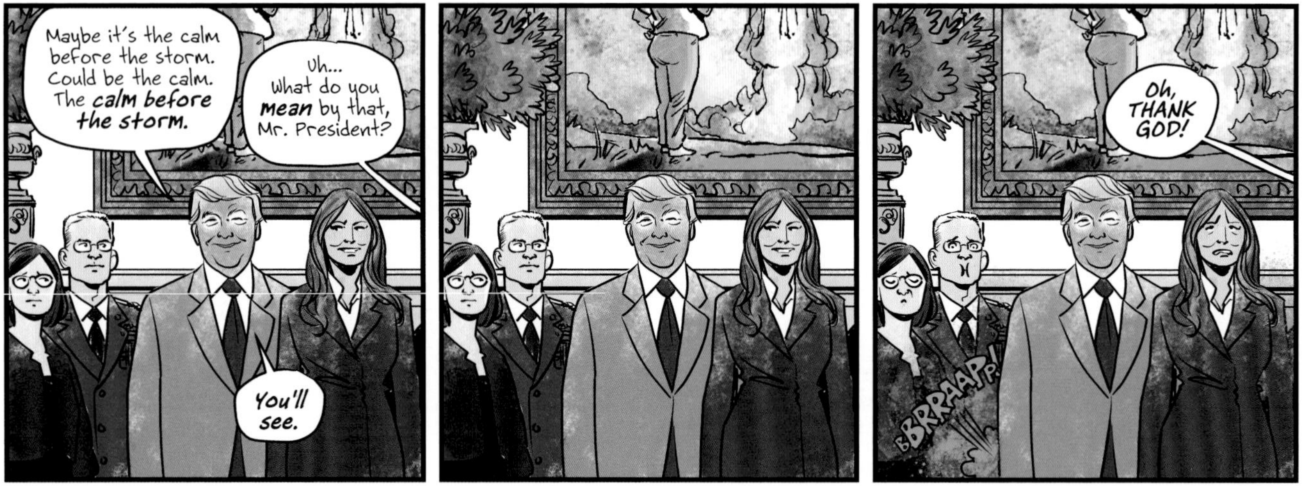
Maybe it's the calm before the storm. Could be the calm. The calm before the storm.
Uh... What do you mean by that, Mr. President?
You'll see.
BRRAAPP!
Oh, THANK GOD!

Oct 11, 2017

Oct 16, 2017

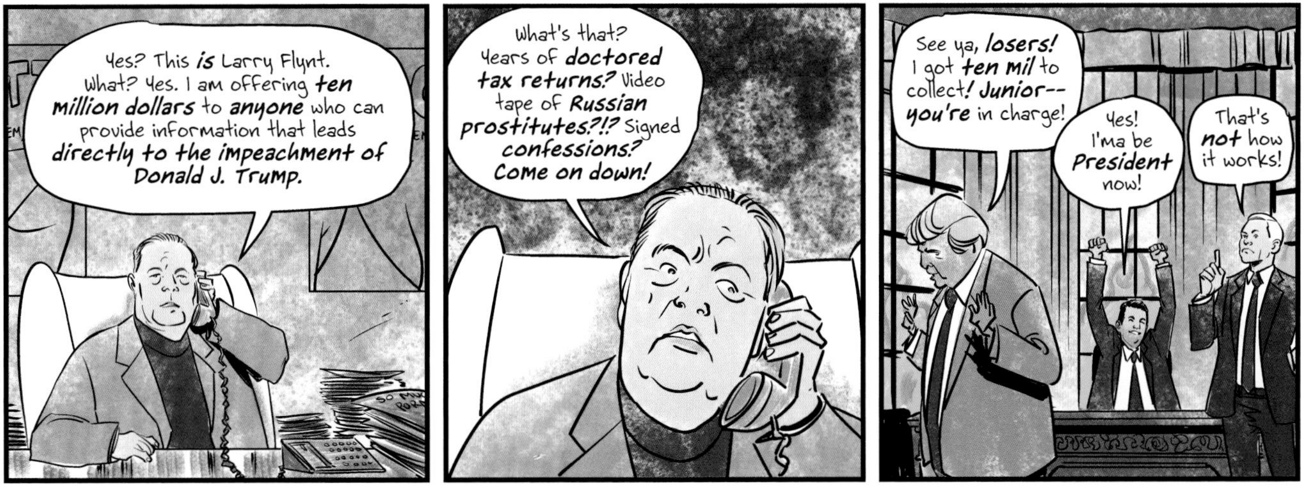
Yes? This is Larry Flynt. What? Yes. I am offering ten million dollars to anyone who can provide information that leads directly to the impeachment of Donald J. Trump.
What's that? Years of doctored tax returns? Video tape of Russian prostitutes?!? Signed confessions? Come on down!
See ya, losers! I got ten mil to collect! Junior-- you're in charge!
Yes! I'ma be President now!
That's not how it works!

Oct 18, 2017

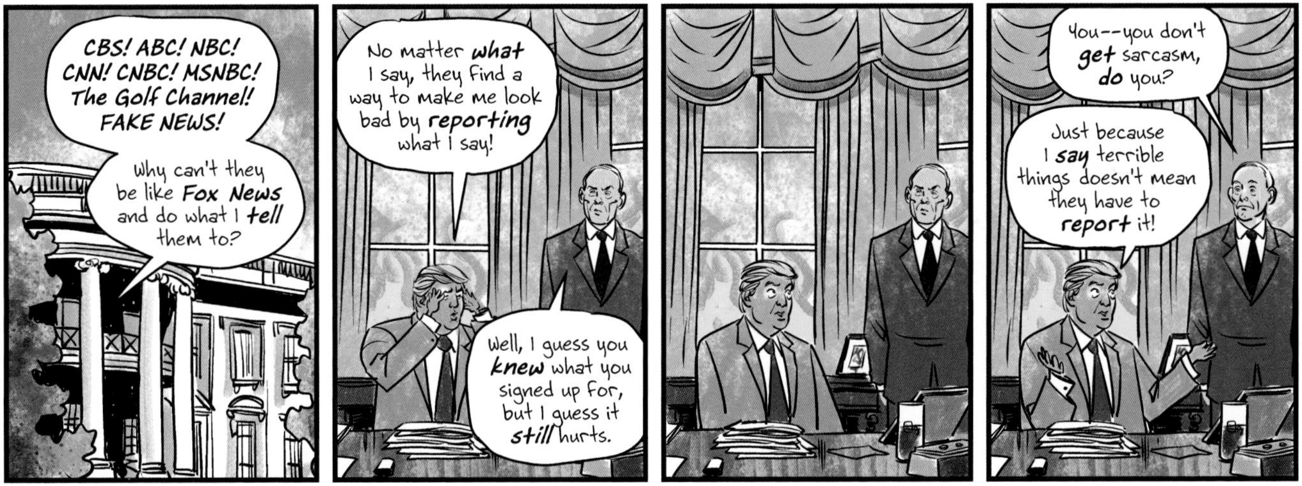
CBS! ABC! NBC! CNN! CNBC! MSNBC! The Golf Channel! FAKE NEWS!
Why can't they be like Fox News and do what I tell them to?
No matter what I say, they find a way to make me look bad by reporting what I say!
Well, I guess you knew what you signed up for, but I guess it still hurts.
You--you don't get sarcasm, do you?
Just because I say terrible things doesn't mean they have to report it!

Oct 23, 2017

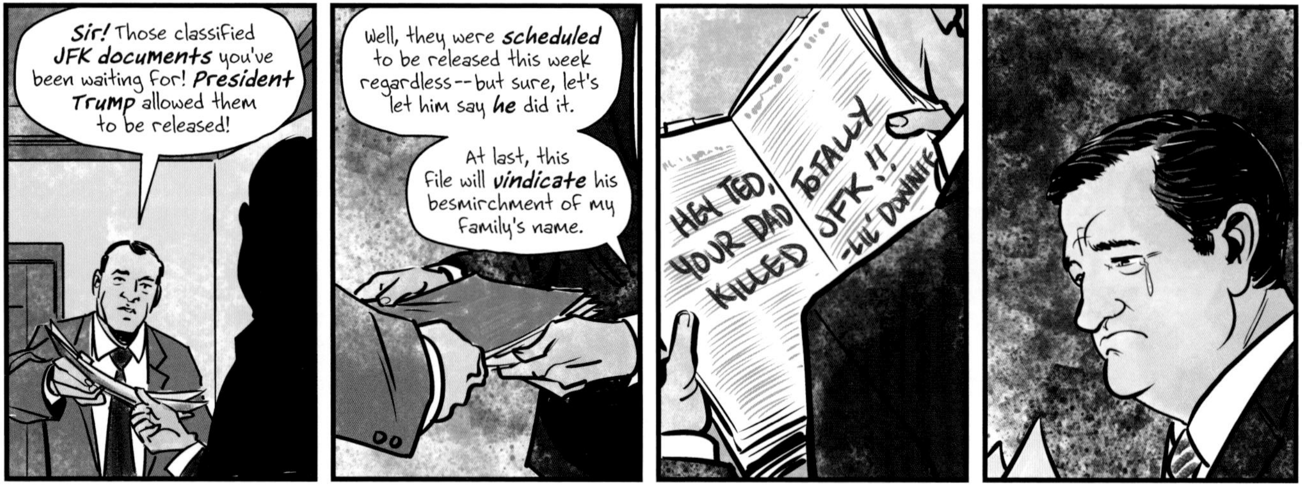
Sir! Those classified JFK documents you've been waiting for! President Trump allowed them to be released!
Well, they were scheduled to be released this week regardless--but sure, let's let him say he did it.
At last, this file will vindicate his besmirchment of my family's name.
HEY TED, YOUR DAD KILLED
TOTALLY JFK!! -LIL' DONNIE

Oct 25, 2017

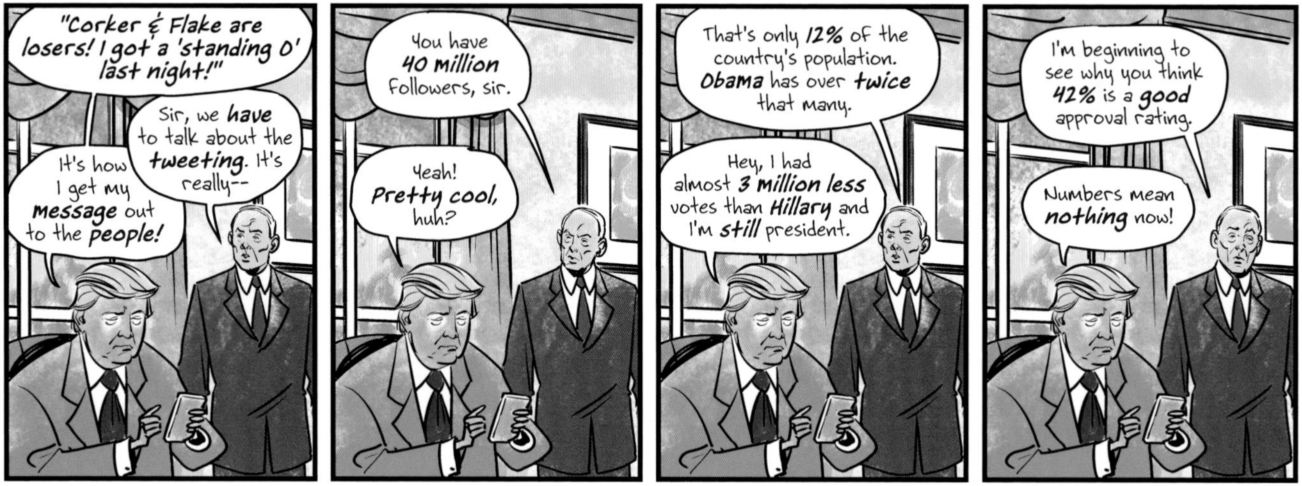
"Corker & Flake are losers! I got a 'standing O' last night!"
Sir, we have to talk about the tweeting. It's really--
It's how I get my message out to the people!
You have 40 million followers, sir.
Yeah! Pretty cool, huh?
That's only 12% of the country's population. Obama has over twice that many.
Hey, I had almost 3 million less votes than Hillary and I'm still president.
I'm beginning to see why you think 42% is a good approval rating.
Numbers mean nothing now!

Oct 30, 2017

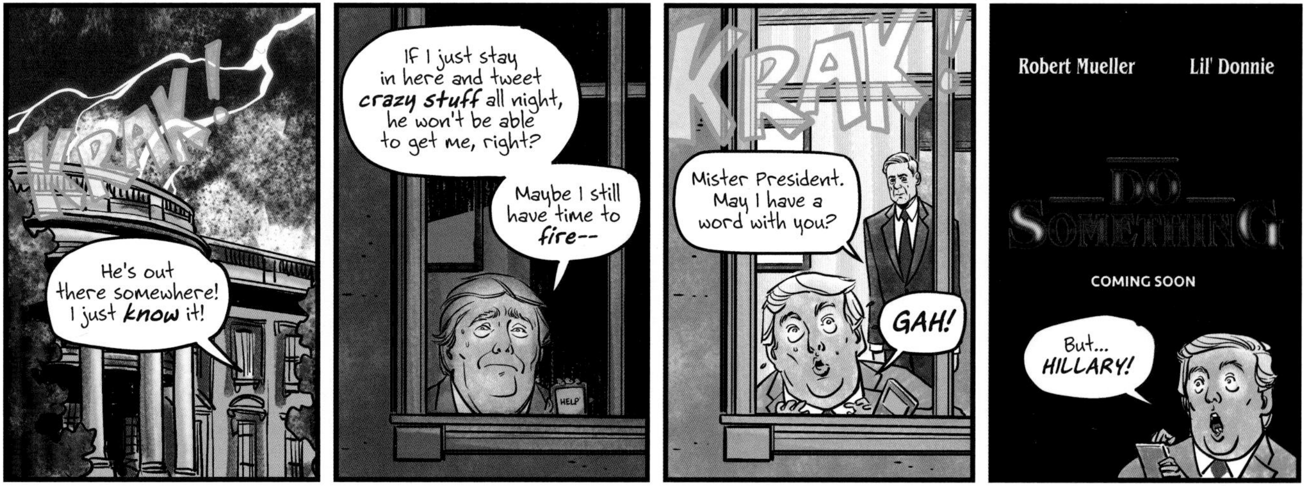
KRAK!
He's out there somewhere! I just **know** it!
If I just stay in here and tweet **crazy stuff** all night, he won't be able to get me, right?
Maybe I still have time to **fire**--
HELP
K'RAK!
Mister President. May I have a word with you?
GAH!
Robert Mueller
Lil' Donnie
DO SOMETHING
COMING SOON
But... **HILLARY!**

Nov 1, 2017

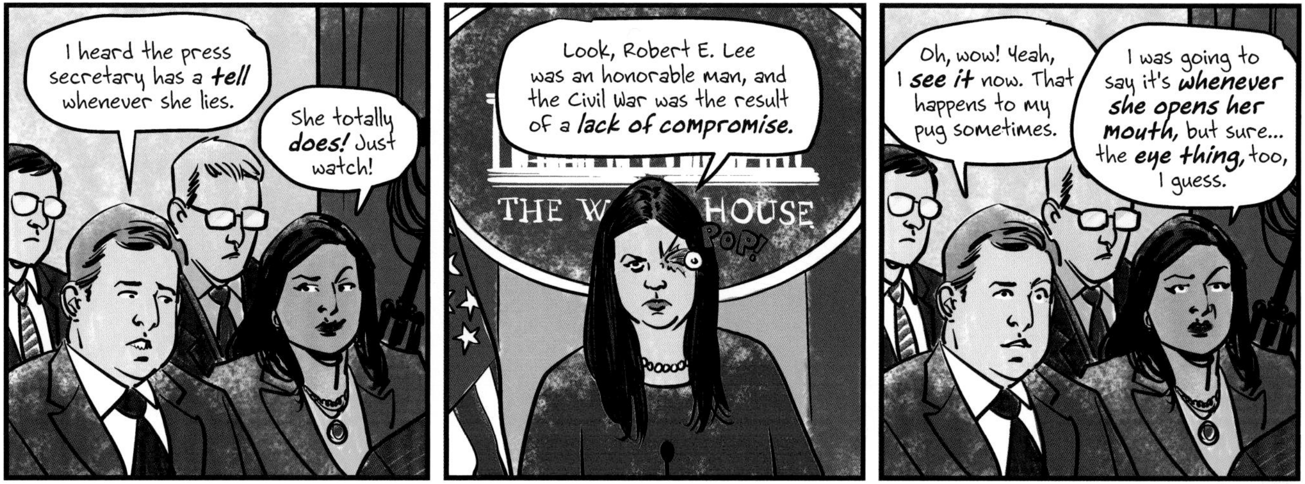
I heard the press secretary has a **tell** whenever she lies.
She totally **does!** Just watch!
Look, Robert E. Lee was an honorable man, and the Civil War was the result of a **lack of compromise.**
POP!
Oh, wow! Yeah, I **see it** now. That happens to my pug sometimes.
I was going to say it's **whenever she opens her mouth,** but sure... the **eye thing,** too, I guess.

Nov 6, 2017

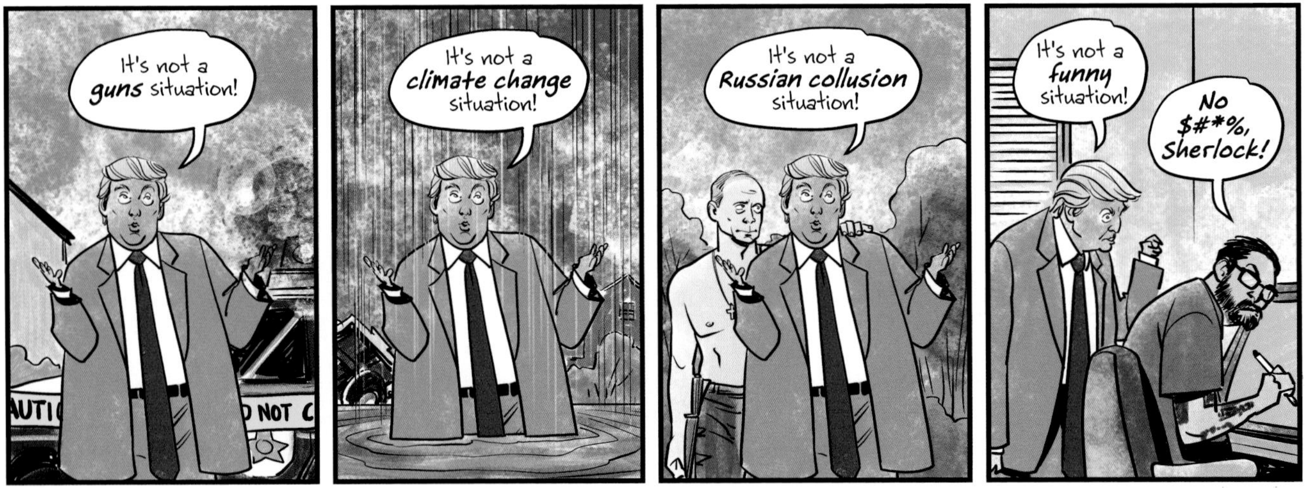
It's not a guns situation!
It's not a climate change situation!
It's not a Russian collusion situation!
It's not a funny situation!
No $#*%, Sherlock!

Nov 10, 2017

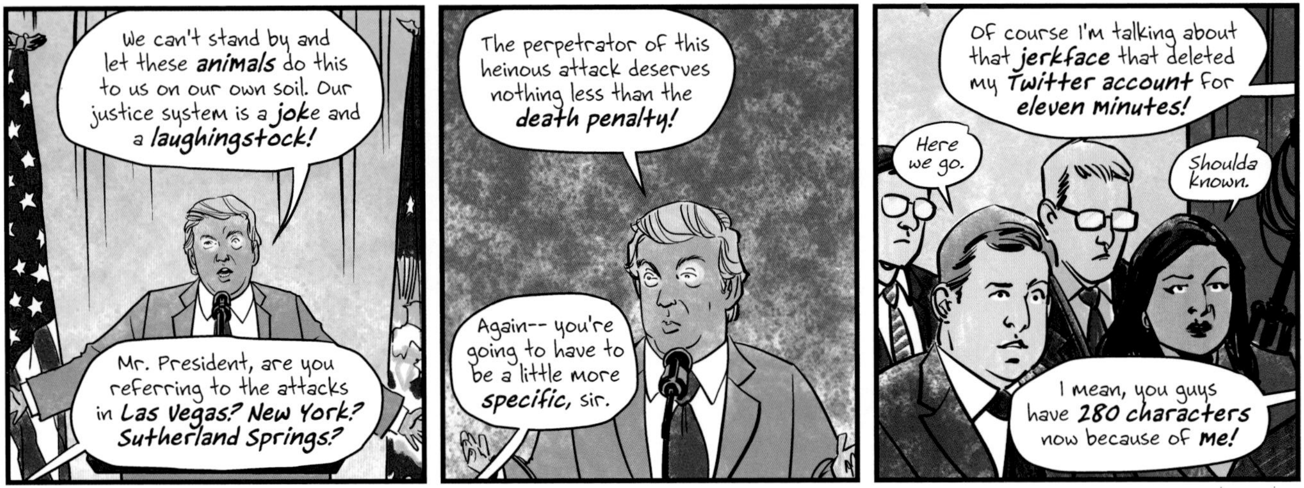
We can't stand by and let these animals do this to us on our own soil. Our justice system is a joke and a laughingstock!
Mr. President, are you referring to the attacks in Las Vegas? New York? Sutherland Springs?
The perpetrator of this heinous attack deserves nothing less than the death penalty!
Again-- you're going to have to be a little more specific, sir.
Of course I'm talking about that jerkface that deleted my Twitter account for eleven minutes!
Here we go.
Shoulda known.
I mean, you guys have 280 characters now because of me!

Nov 13, 2017

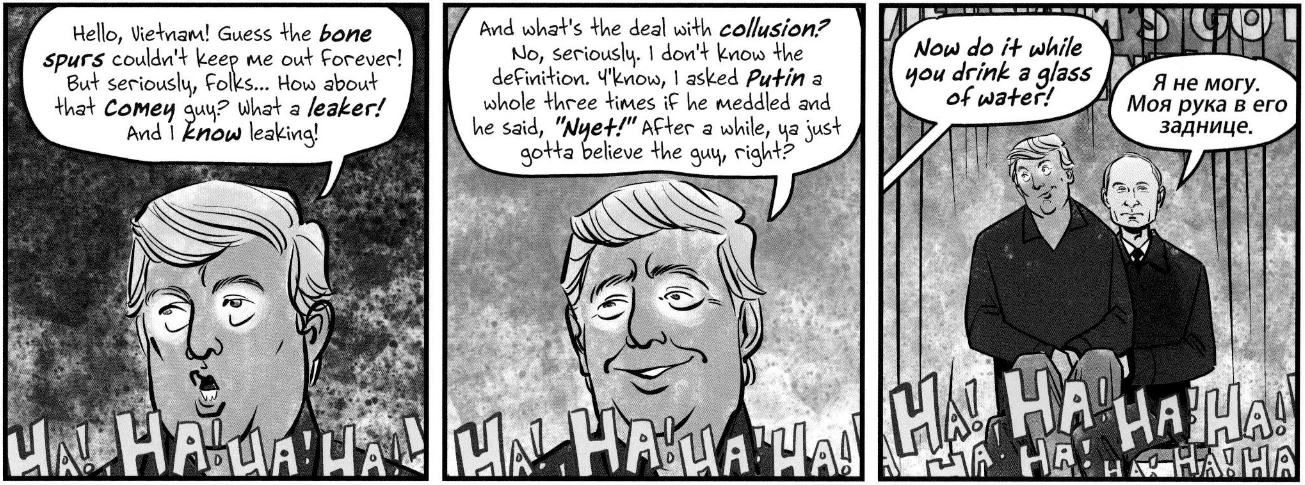
Hello, Vietnam! Guess the **bone spurs** couldn't keep me out forever! But seriously, folks... How about that **Comey** guy? What a **leaker!** And I **know** leaking!
HA! HA! HA! HA!
And what's the deal with **collusion?** No, seriously. I don't know the definition. Y'know, I asked **Putin** a whole three times if he meddled and he said, **"Nyet!"** After a while, ya just gotta believe the guy, right?
HA! HA! HA! HA!
Now do it while you drink a glass of water!
Я не могу. Моя рука в его заднице.
HA! HA! HA! HA!
HA! HA! HA! HA!

Nov 15, 2017

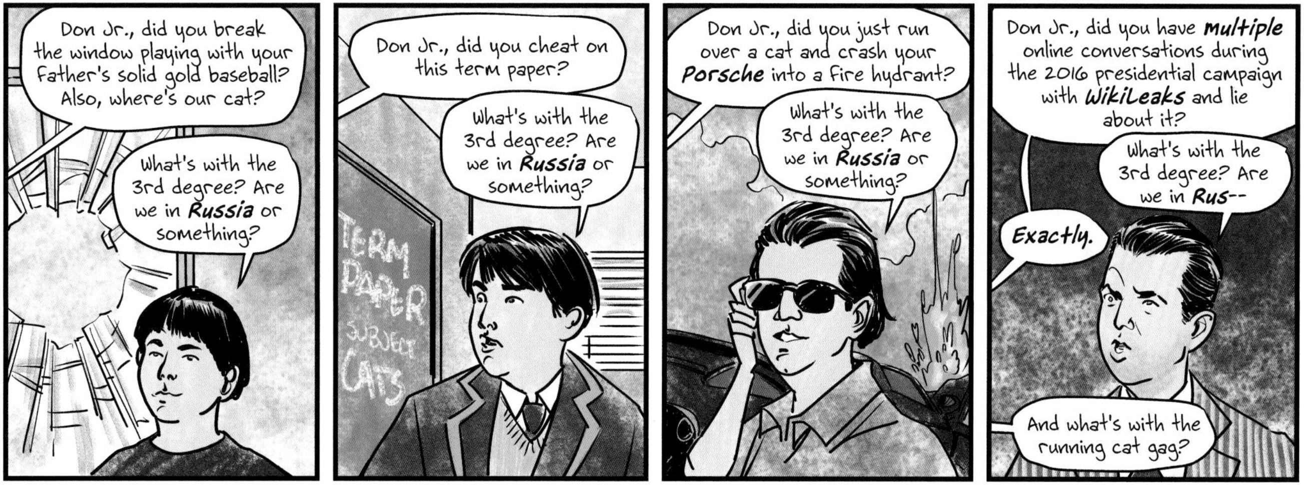
Don Jr., did you break the window playing with your father's solid gold baseball? Also, where's our cat?
What's with the 3rd degree? Are we in **Russia** or something?
Don Jr., did you cheat on this term paper?
What's with the 3rd degree? Are we in **Russia** or something?
TERM PAPER
SUBJECT
CATS
Don Jr., did you just run over a cat and crash your **Porsche** into a fire hydrant?
What's with the 3rd degree? Are we in **Russia** or something?
Don Jr., did you have **multiple** online conversations during the 2016 presidential campaign with **WikiLeaks** and lie about it?
What's with the 3rd degree? Are we in **Rus**--
Exactly.
And what's with the running cat gag?

Nov 21, 2017

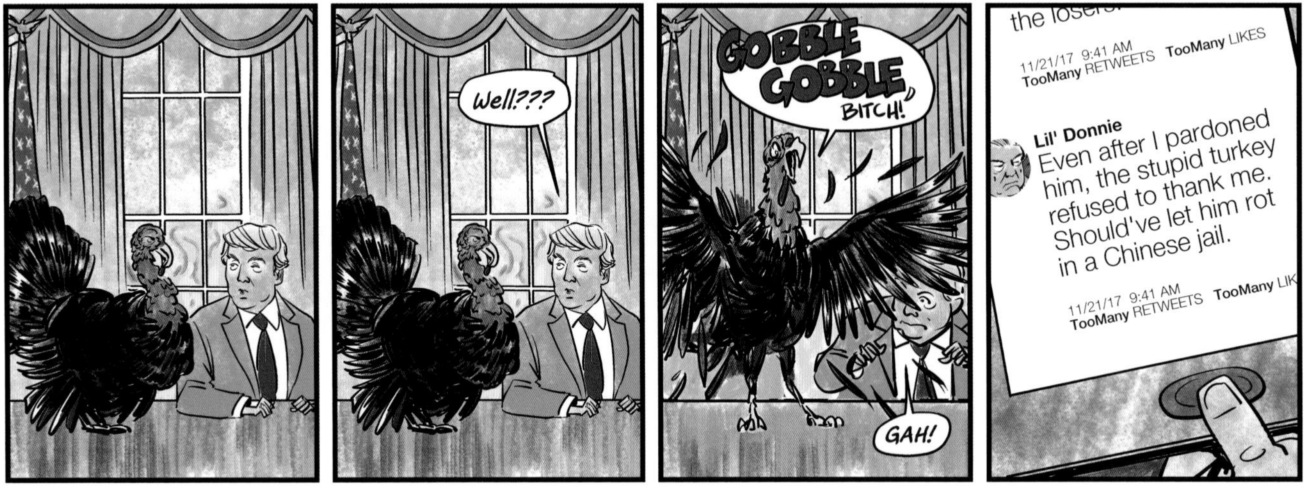
Well???
GOBBLE GOBBLE, BITCH!
GAH!
11/21/17 9:41 AM TooMany RETWEETS TooMany LIKES
Lil' Donnie
Even after I pardoned him, the stupid turkey refused to thank me. Should've let him rot in a Chinese jail.
11/21/17 9:41 AM TooMany RETWEETS TooMany

Nov 27, 2017

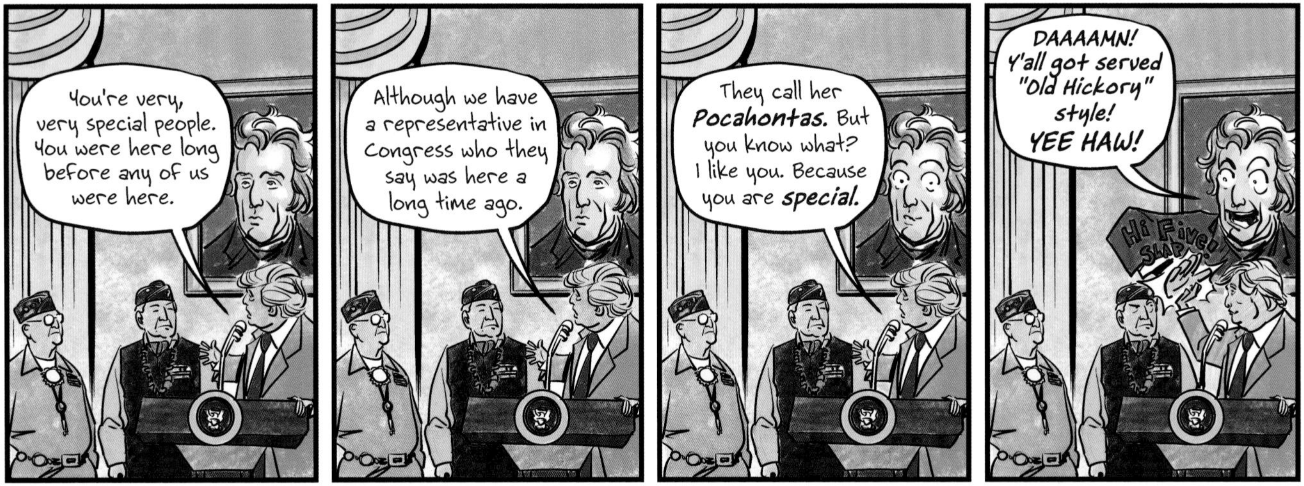
You're very, very special people. You were here long before any of us were here.
Although we have a representative in Congress who they say was here a long time ago.
They call her Pocahontas. But you know what? I like you. Because you are special.
DAAAAMN! Y'all got served "Old Hickory" style! YEE HAW!
Hi Five!
SLAP!

Dec 2, 2017

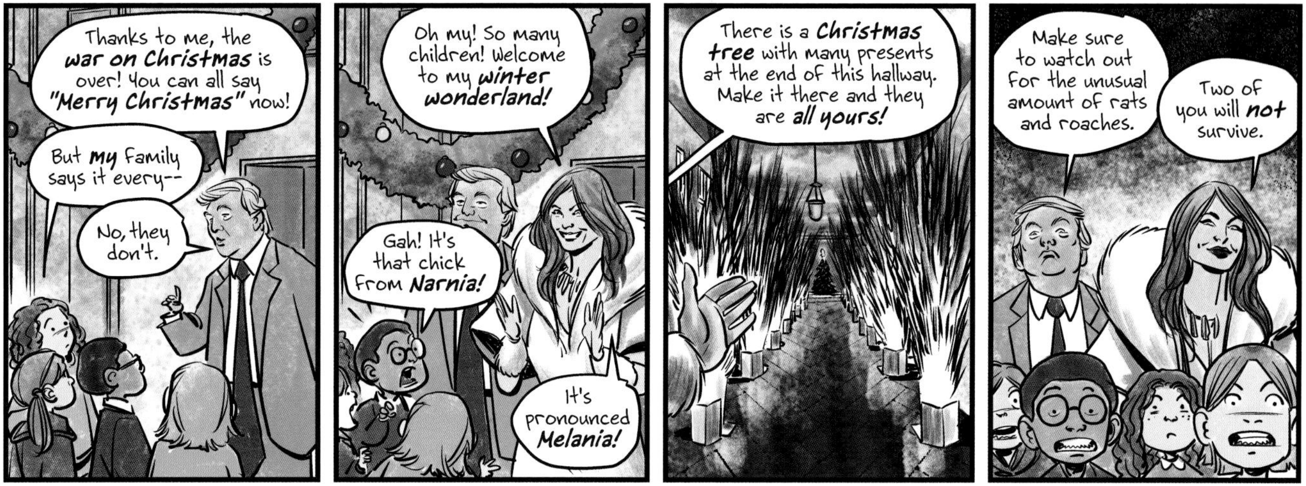

Thanks to me, the war on Christmas is over! You can all say "Merry Christmas" now!
But my family says it every--
No, they don't.
Oh my! So many children! Welcome to my winter wonderland!
Gah! It's that chick from Narnia!
It's pronounced Melania!
There is a Christmas tree with many presents at the end of this hallway. Make it there and they are all yours!
Make sure to watch out for the unusual amount of rats and roaches.
Two of you will not survive.

Dec 4, 2017

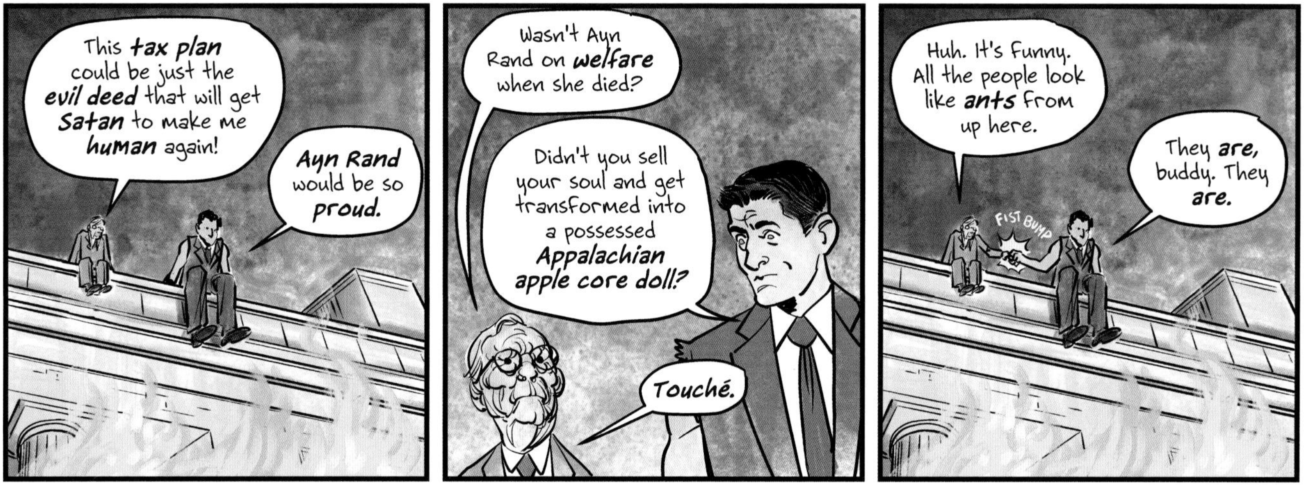

This tax plan could be just the evil deed that will get Satan to make me human again!
Ayn Rand would be so proud.
Wasn't Ayn Rand on welfare when she died?
Didn't you sell your soul and get transformed into a possessed Appalachian apple core doll?
Touché.
Huh. It's funny. All the people look like ants from up here.
FIST BUMP
They are, buddy. They are.

Dec 6, 2017

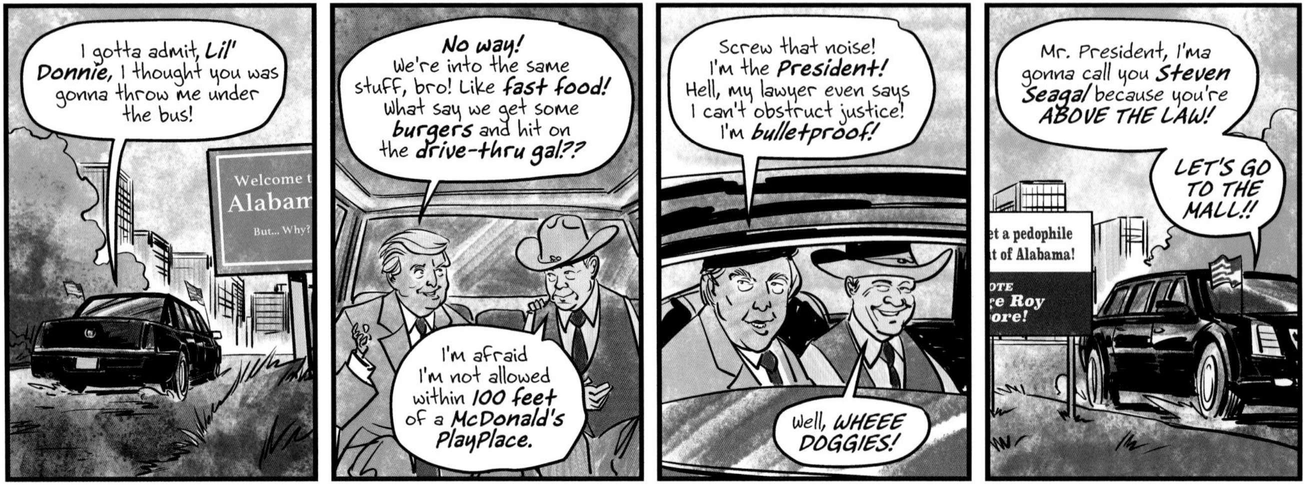
I gotta admit, Lil' Donnie, I thought you was gonna throw me under the bus!
Welcome t
Alabam
But... Why?
No way! We're into the same stuff, bro! Like fast food! What say we get some burgers and hit on the drive-thru gal??
I'm afraid I'm not allowed within 100 feet of a McDonald's PlayPlace.
Screw that noise! I'm the President! Hell, my lawyer even says I can't obstruct justice! I'm bulletproof!
Well, WHEEE DOGGIES!
Mr. President, I'ma gonna call you Steven Seagal because you're ABOVE THE LAW!
LET'S GO TO THE MALL!!
et a pedophile
t of Alabama!
OTE
e Roy
ore!

Dec 11, 2017

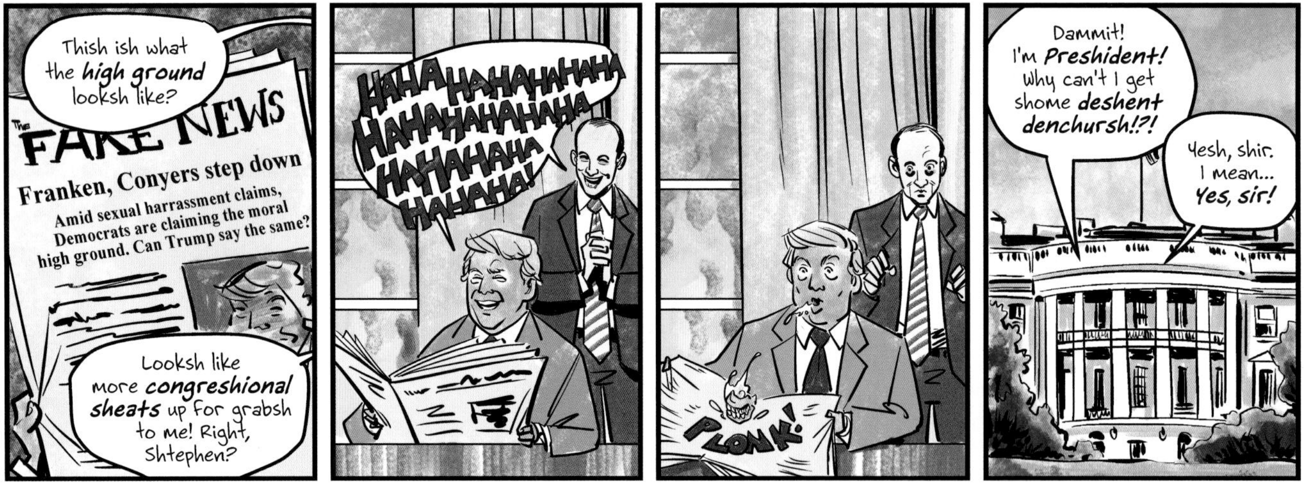
Thish ish what the high ground looksh like?
The FAKE NEWS
Franken, Conyers step down
Franken, Conyers step down
Amid sexual harrassment claims, Democrats are claiming the moral high ground. Can Trump say the same?
Looksh like more congreshional sheats up for grabsh to me! Right, Shtephen?
HAHAHAHAHAHAHA HAHAHAHAHAHAHA HAHAHAHA HAHAHA!
PLONK!
Dammit! I'm Preshident! Why can't I get shome deshent denchursh!?!
Yesh, shir. I mean... Yes, sir!

Lil' Do

Dec 14, 2017

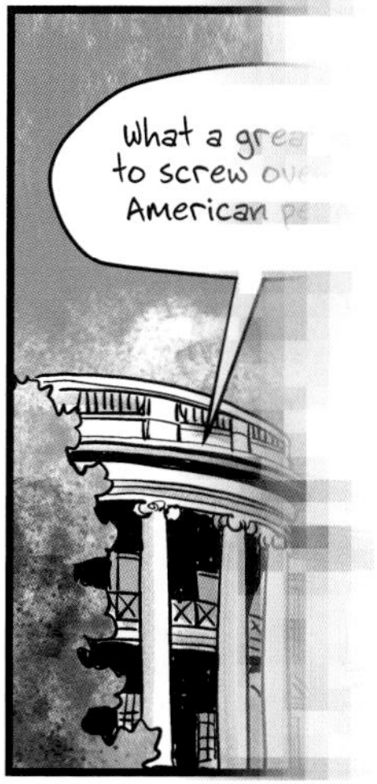
What a
to screw
American

lildonniecomic.com

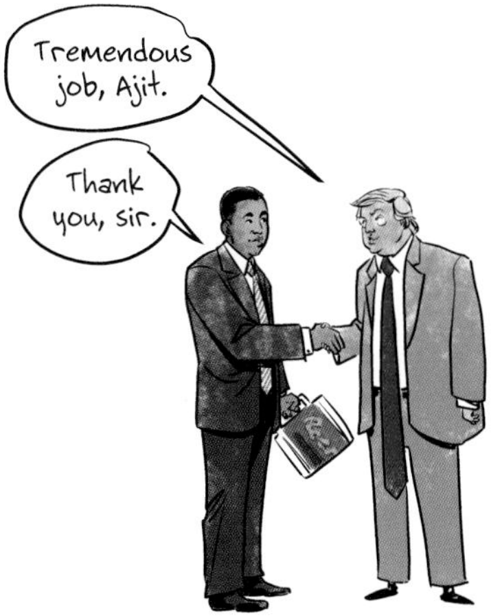
Tremendous job, Ajit.
Thank you, sir.

Dec 18, 2017

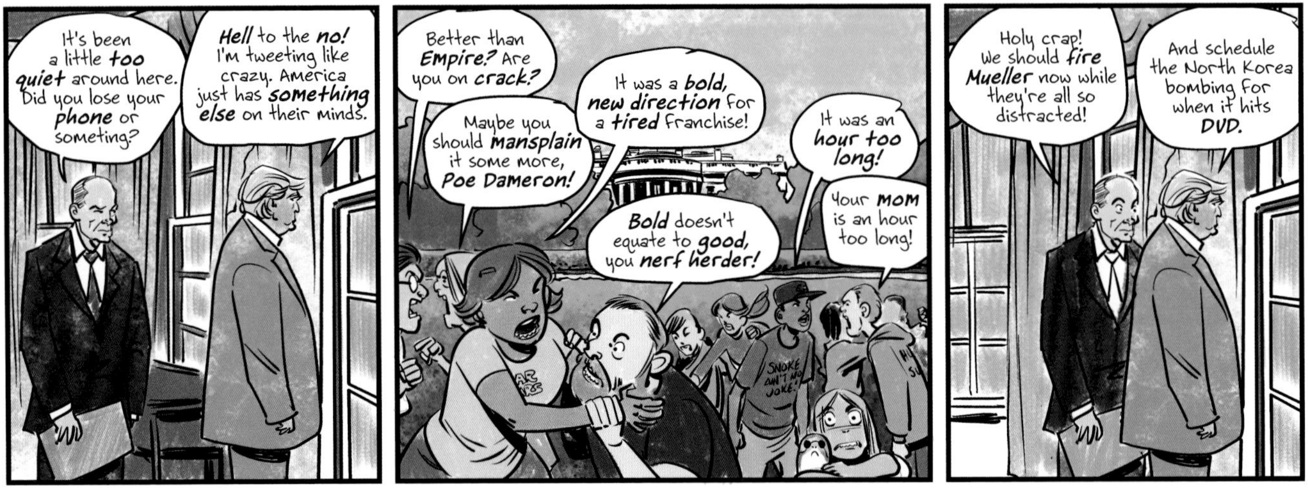

It's been a little **too quiet** around here. Did you lose your **phone** or someting?
Hell to the **no!** I'm tweeting like crazy. America just has **something else** on their minds.
Better than **Empire?** Are you on **crack?**
Maybe you should **mansplain** it some more, **Poe Dameron!**
It was a **bold, new direction** for a **tired** franchise!
Bold doesn't equate to **good,** you **nerf herder!**
It was an **hour too long!**
Your **MOM** is an hour too long!
Holy crap! We should **fire Mueller** now while they're all so distracted!
And schedule the North Korea bombing for when it hits **DVD.**

Dec 22, 2017

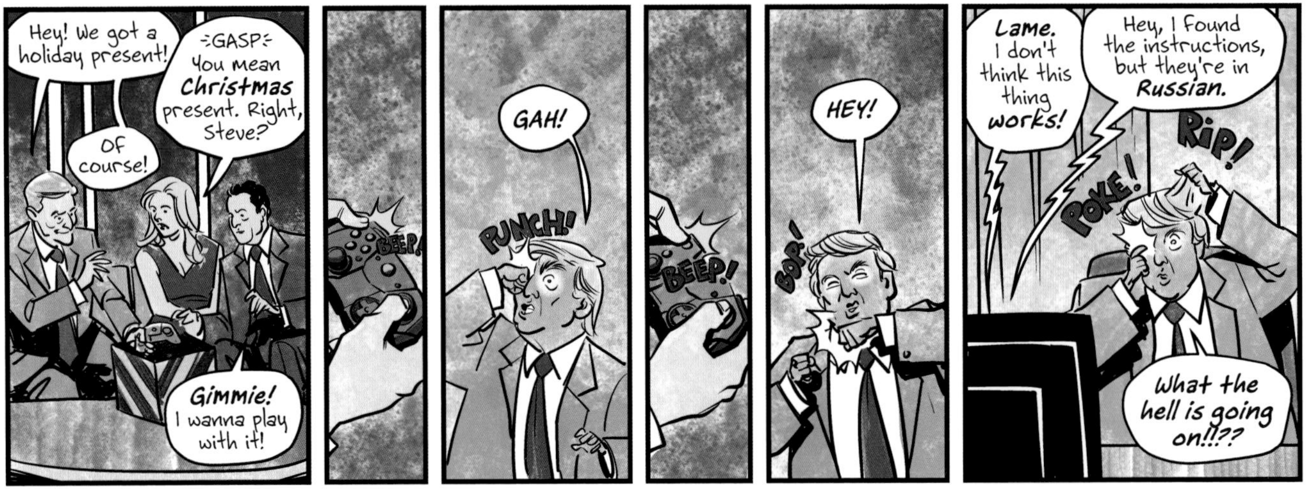

Hey! We got a holiday present!
Of course!
GASP You mean **Christmas** present. Right, Steve?
Gimmie! I wanna play with it!
BEEP!
PUNCH!
GAH!
BEEP!
BOP!
HEY!
Lame. I don't think this thing **works!**
Hey, I found the instructions, but they're in **Russian.**
POKE!
RIP!
What the hell is going on!!??

Jan 2, 2018

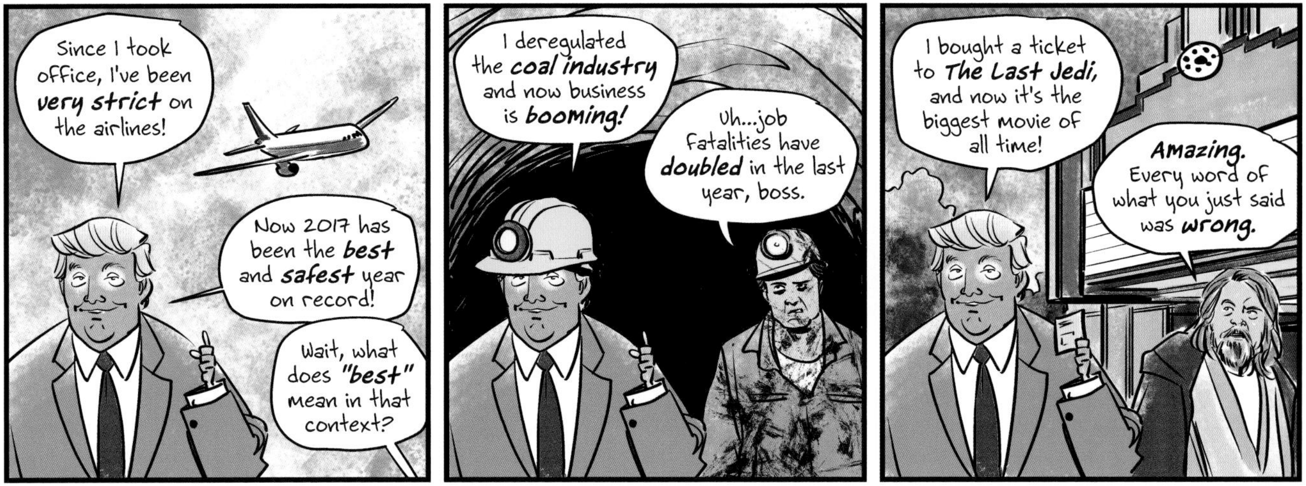
Since I took office, I've been very strict on the airlines!
Now 2017 has been the best and safest year on record!
Wait, what does "best" mean in that context?
I deregulated the coal industry and now business is booming!
Uh...job fatalities have doubled in the last year, boss.
I bought a ticket to The Last Jedi, and now it's the biggest movie of all time!
Amazing. Every word of what you just said was wrong.

Jan 5, 2018

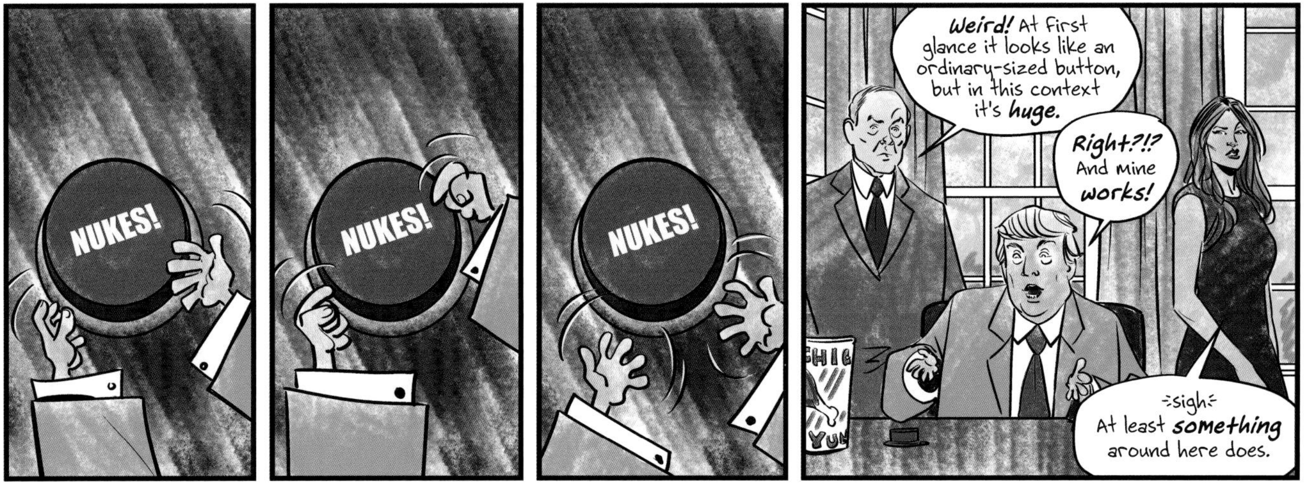
NUKES!
NUKES!
NUKES!
Weird! At first glance it looks like an ordinary-sized button, but in this context it's huge.
Right?!? And mine works!
sigh
At least something around here does.

Jan 8, 2018

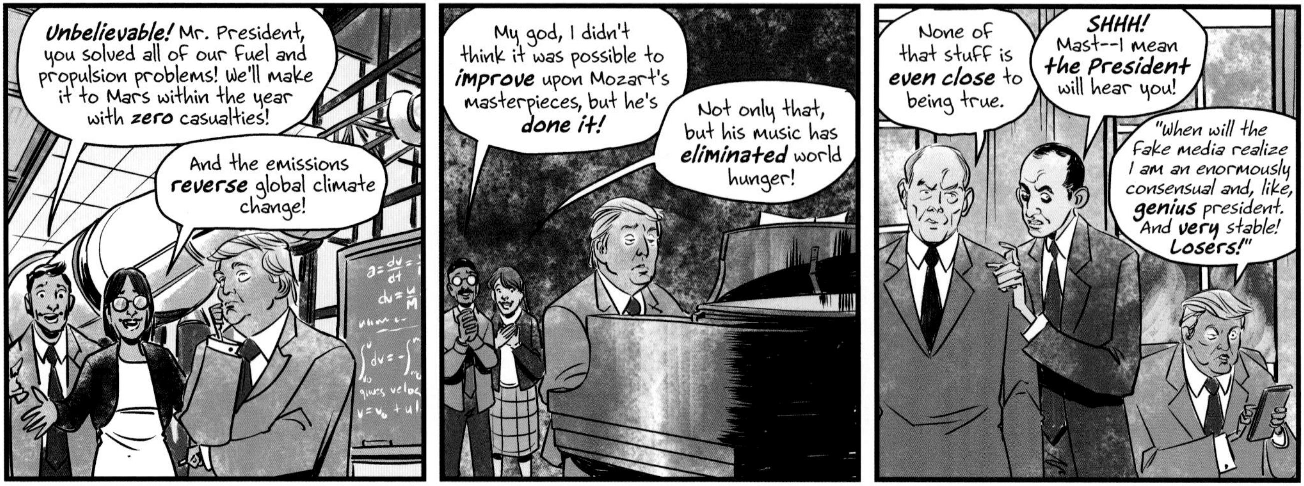

Unbelievable! Mr. President, you solved all of our fuel and propulsion problems! We'll make it to Mars within the year with zero casualties!
And the emissions reverse global climate change!
My god, I didn't think it was possible to improve upon Mozart's masterpieces, but he's done it!
Not only that, but his music has eliminated world hunger!
None of that stuff is even close to being true.
SHHH! Mast--I mean the President will hear you!
"When will the fake media realize I am an enormously consensual and, like, genius president. And very stable! Losers!"

Jan 12, 2018

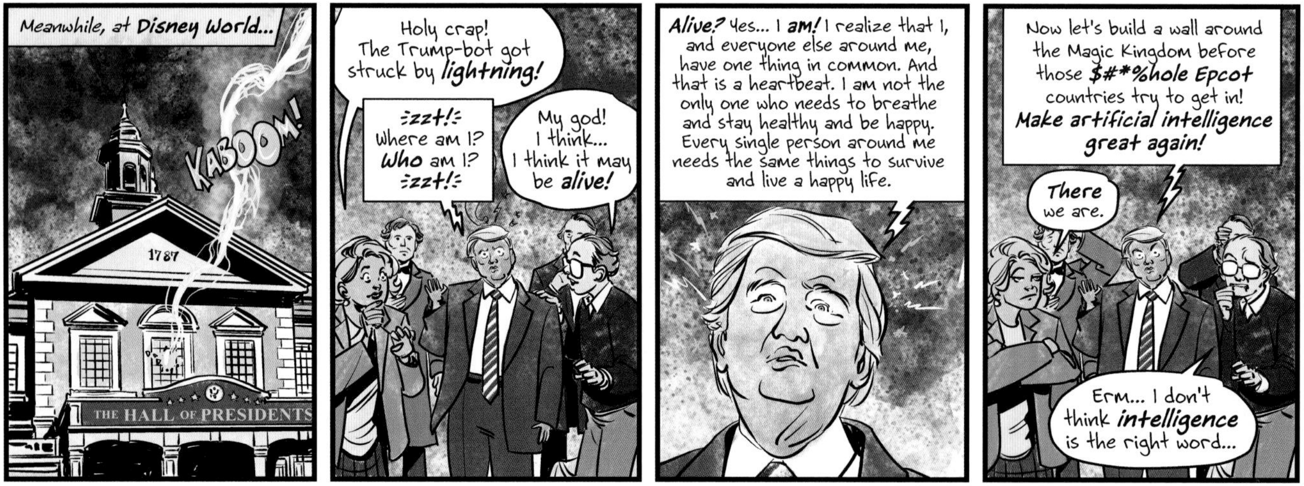

Meanwhile, at Disney World...
KABOOM!
1787
THE HALL OF PRESIDENTS
Holy crap! The Trump-bot got struck by lightning!
=zzt!= Where am I? Who am I? =zzt!=
My god! I think... I think it may be alive!
Alive? Yes... I am! I realize that I, and everyone else around me, have one thing in common. And that is a heartbeat. I am not the only one who needs to breathe and stay healthy and be happy. Every single person around me needs the same things to survive and live a happy life.
Now let's build a wall around the Magic Kingdom before those $#*%hole Epcot countries try to get in! Make artificial intelligence great again!
There we are.
Erm... I don't think intelligence is the right word...

Jan 15, 2018

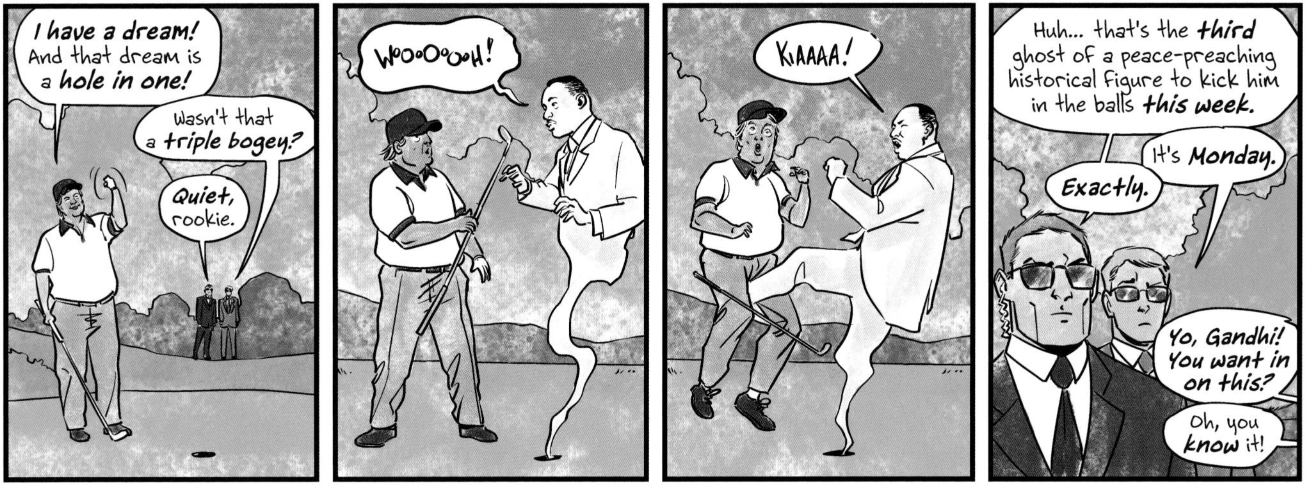
I have a dream! And that dream is a hole in one!
Wasn't that a triple bogey?
Quiet, rookie.
WoOoOoOOH!
KIAAAA!
Huh... that's the third ghost of a peace-preaching historical figure to kick him in the balls this week.
It's Monday.
Exactly.
Yo, Gandhi! You want in on this?
Oh, you know it!

Jan 19, 2018

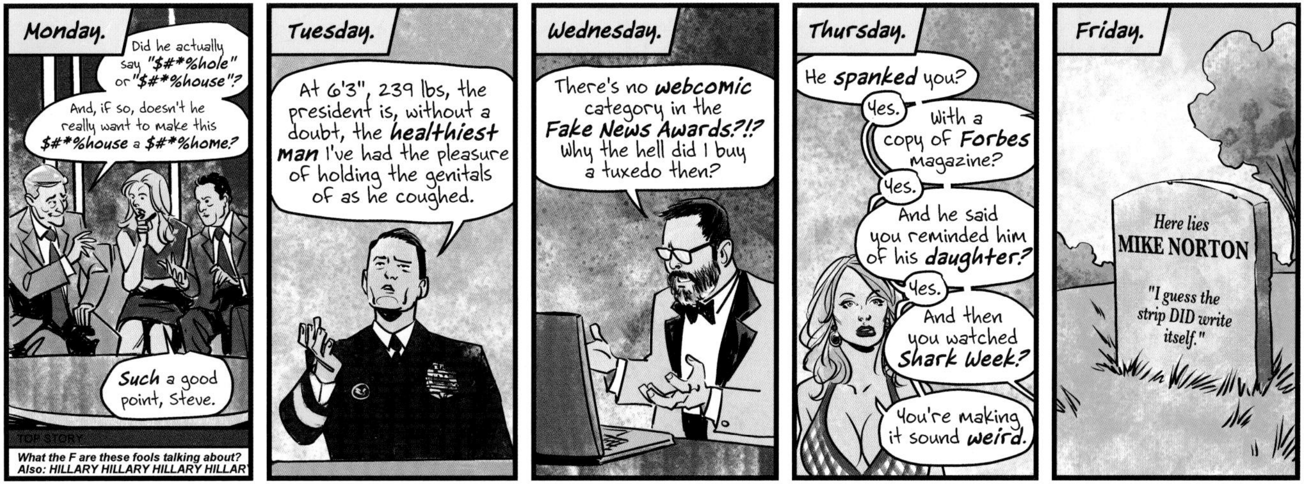
Monday.
Did he actually say "$#*%hole" or "$#*%house"?
And, if so, doesn't he really want to make this $#*%house a $#*%home?
Such a good point, Steve.
TOP STORY
What the F are these fools talking about?
Also: HILLARY HILLARY HILLARY HILLAR
Tuesday.
At 6'3", 239 lbs, the president is, without a doubt, the healthiest man I've had the pleasure of holding the genitals of as he coughed.
Wednesday.
There's no webcomic category in the Fake News Awards?!? Why the hell did I buy a tuxedo then?
Thursday.
He spanked you?
Yes.
With a copy of Forbes magazine?
Yes.
And he said you reminded him of his daughter?
Yes.
And then you watched Shark Week?
You're making it sound weird.
Friday.
Here lies
MIKE NORTON
"I guess the strip DID write itself."

Jan 29, 2018

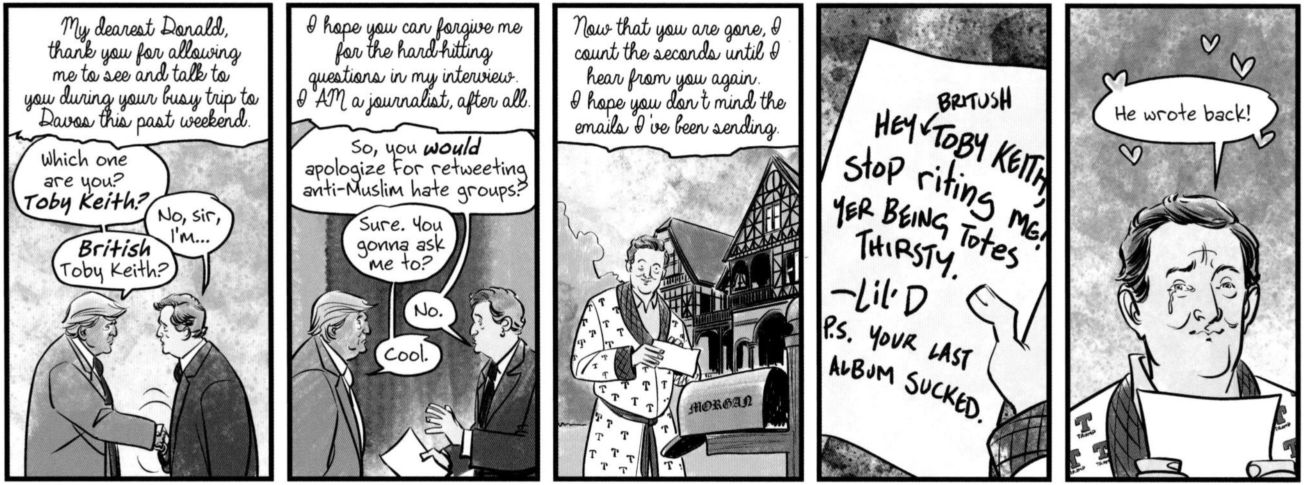

My dearest Donald, thank you for allowing me to see and talk to you during your busy trip to Davos this past weekend.
Which one are you? Toby Keith?
No, sir, I'm...
British Toby Keith?
I hope you can forgive me for the hard-hitting questions in my interview. I AM a journalist, after all.
So, you would apologize for retweeting anti-Muslim hate groups?
Sure. You gonna ask me to?
No.
Cool.
Now that you are gone, I count the seconds until I hear from you again. I hope you don't mind the emails I've been sending.
MORGAN
HEY BRITUSH TOBY KEITH, STOP RITING ME! YER BEING TOTES THIRSTY.
—LIL' D
P.S. YOUR LAST ALBUM SUCKED.
He wrote back!

Feb 2, 2018

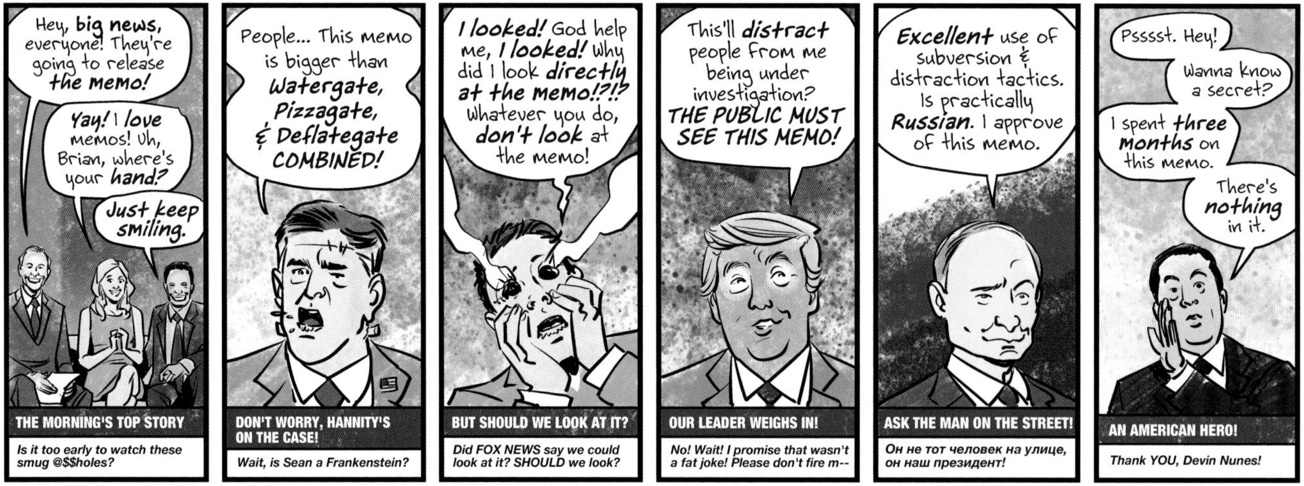

Hey, big news, everyone! They're going to release the memo!
Yay! I love memos! Uh, Brian, where's your hand?
Just keep smiling.
THE MORNING'S TOP STORY
Is it too early to watch these smug @$$holes?
People... This memo is bigger than Watergate, Pizzagate, & Deflategate COMBINED!
DON'T WORRY, HANNITY'S ON THE CASE!
Wait, is Sean a Frankenstein?
I looked! God help me, I looked! Why did I look directly at the memo!?!? Whatever you do, don't look at the memo!
BUT SHOULD WE LOOK AT IT?
Did FOX NEWS say we could look at it? SHOULD we look?
This'll distract people from me being under investigation? THE PUBLIC MUST SEE THIS MEMO!
OUR LEADER WEIGHS IN!
No! Wait! I promise that wasn't a fat joke! Please don't fire m--
Excellent use of subversion & distraction tactics. Is practically Russian. I approve of this memo.
ASK THE MAN ON THE STREET!
Он не тот человек на улице, он наш президент!
Psssst. Hey!
Wanna know a secret?
I spent three months on this memo.
There's nothing in it.
AN AMERICAN HERO!
Thank YOU, Devin Nunes!

Feb 5, 2018

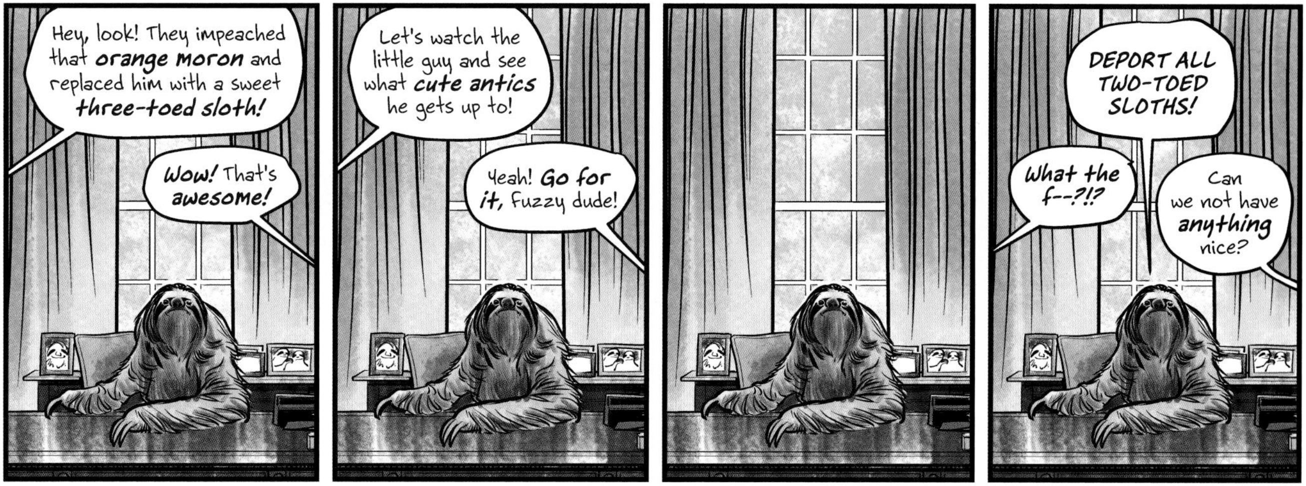

Hey, look! They impeached that orange moron and replaced him with a sweet three-toed sloth!
Wow! That's awesome!
Let's watch the little guy and see what cute antics he gets up to!
Yeah! Go for it, Fuzzy dude!
DEPORT ALL TWO-TOED SLOTHS!
What the f--?!?
Can we not have anything nice?

Feb 7, 2018

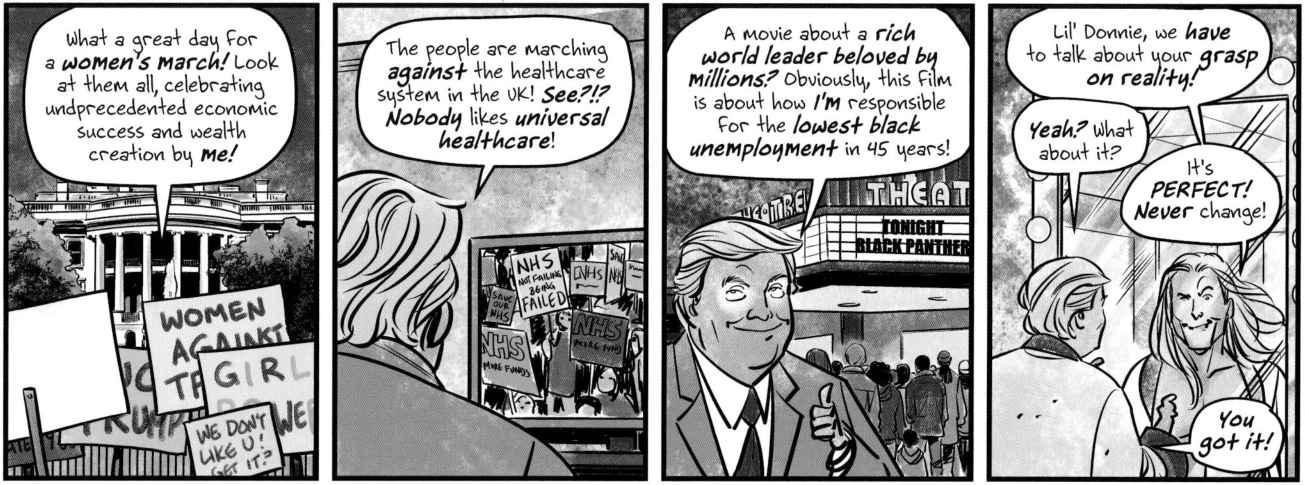

What a great day for a women's march! Look at them all, celebrating undprecedented economic success and wealth creation by me!
WOMEN
WE DON'T LIKE U!
The people are marching against the healthcare system in the UK! See?!? Nobody likes universal healthcare!
NHS NOT FAILING BEING FAILED
SAVE OUR NHS
NHS MORE FUNDS
A movie about a rich world leader beloved by millions? Obviously, this film is about how I'M responsible for the lowest black unemployment in 45 years!
TONIGHT BLACK PANTHER
Lil' Donnie, we have to talk about your grasp on reality!
Yeah? What about it?
It's PERFECT! Never change!
You got it!

Feb 9, 2018

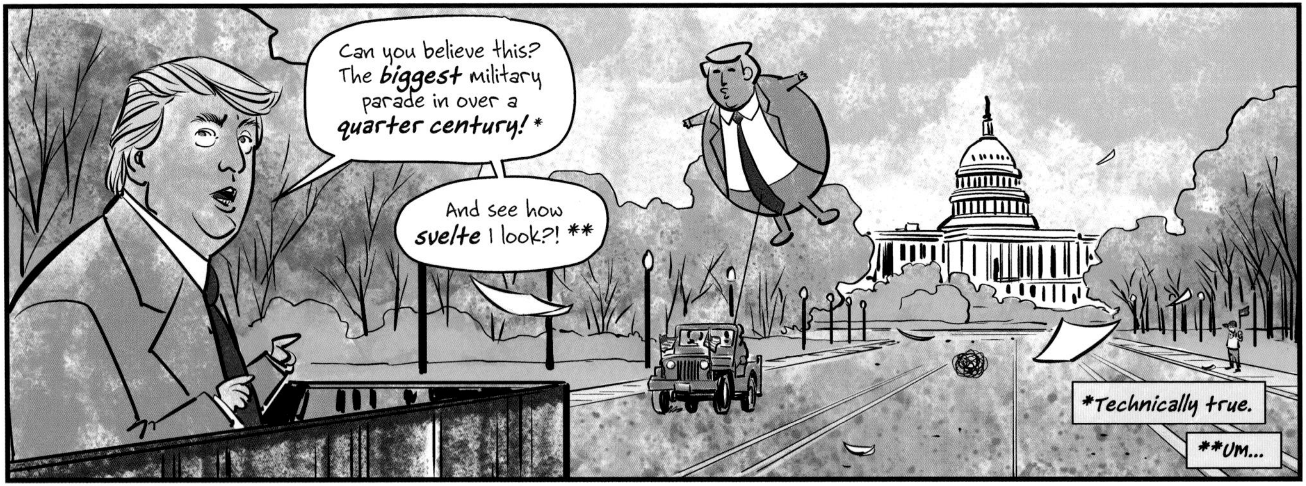

Can you believe this? The **biggest** military parade in over a **quarter century!** *
And see how **svelte** I look?! **
*Technically true.
**UM...

Feb 12, 2018

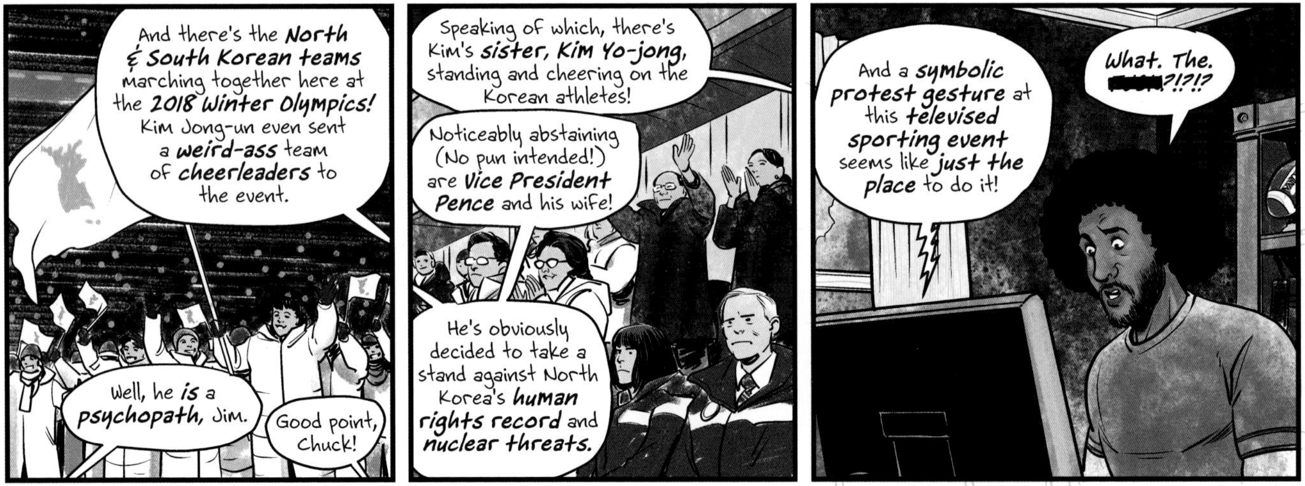

And there's the **North & South Korean teams** marching together here at the **2018 Winter Olympics!** Kim Jong-un even sent a **weird-ass** team of **cheerleaders** to the event.
Well, he **is** a **psychopath,** Jim.
Good point, Chuck!
Speaking of which, there's Kim's **sister, Kim Yo-jong,** standing and cheering on the Korean athletes!
Noticeably abstaining (No pun intended!) are **Vice President Pence** and his wife!
He's obviously decided to take a stand against North Korea's **human rights record** and **nuclear threats.**
And a **symbolic protest gesture** at this **televised sporting event** seems like **just the place** to do it!
What. The. [redacted]?!?!?

Feb 15, 2018

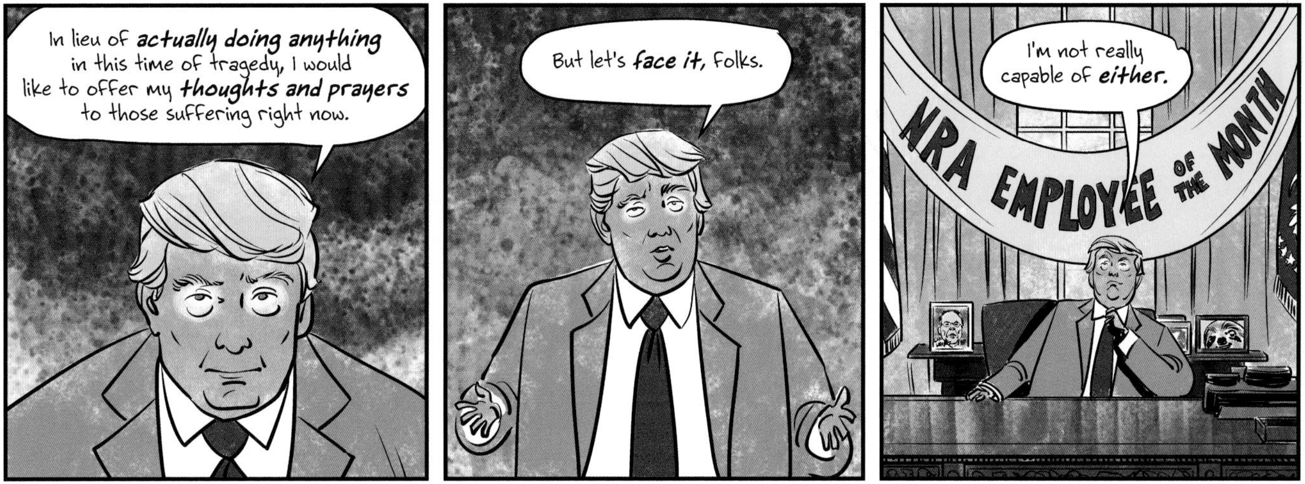
In lieu of actually doing anything in this time of tragedy, I would like to offer my thoughts and prayers to those suffering right now.
But let's face it, folks.
NRA EMPLOYEE OF THE MONTH
I'm not really capable of either.

Mar 5, 2018

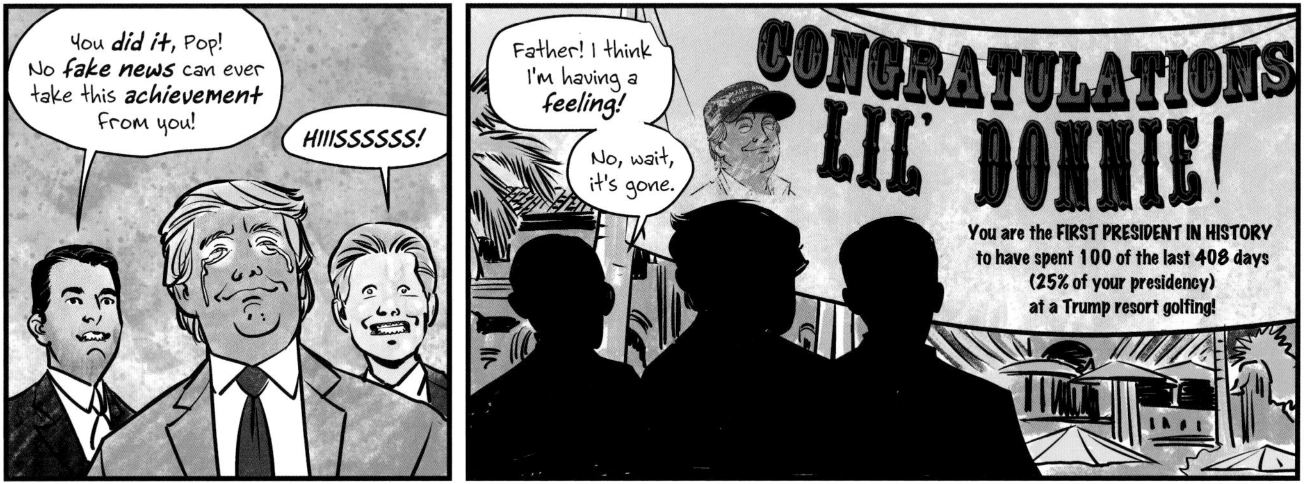
You did it, Pop! No fake news can ever take this achievement from you!
HIIISSSSSS!
CONGRATULATIONS LIL' DONNIE!
You are the FIRST PRESIDENT IN HISTORY to have spent 100 of the last 408 days (25% of your presidency) at a Trump resort golfing!
Father! I think I'm having a feeling!
No, wait, it's gone.

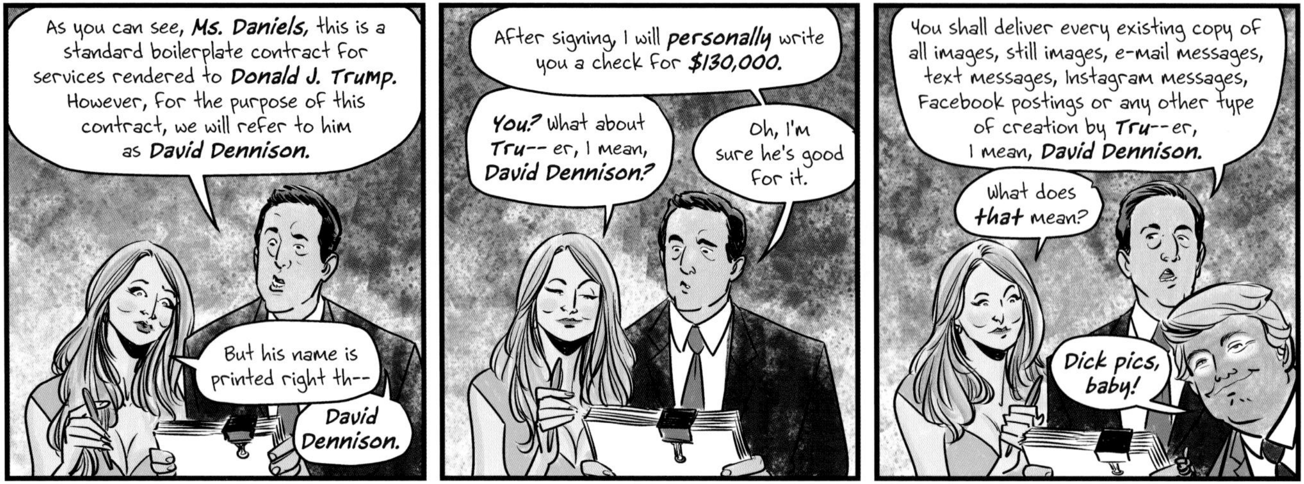
As you can see, **Ms. Daniels,** this is a standard boilerplate contract for services rendered to **Donald J. Trump.** However, for the purpose of this contract, we will refer to him as **David Dennison.**
But his name is printed right th--
David Dennison.
After signing, I will **personally** write you a check for **$130,000.**
You? What about **Tru--** er, I mean, **David Dennison?**
Oh, I'm sure he's good for it.
You shall deliver every existing copy of all images, still images, e-mail messages, text messages, Instagram messages, Facebook postings or any other type of creation by **Tru--**er, I mean, **David Dennison.**
What does **that** mean?
Dick pics, baby!

Mar 7, 2018

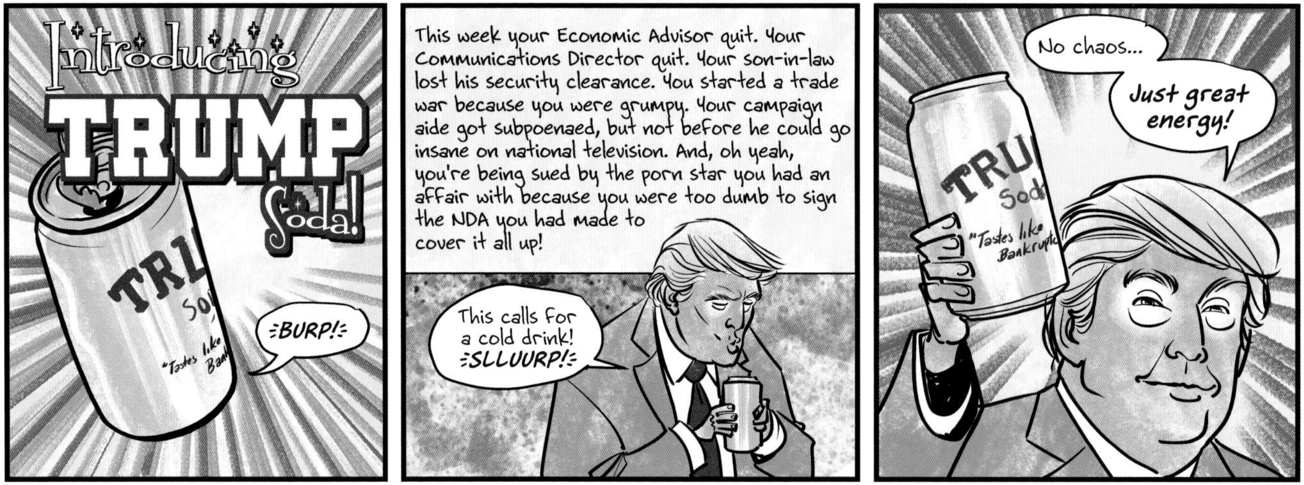
Introducing
TRUMP
Soda!
TRU
So
"Tastes like Ban
BURP!
This week your Economic Advisor quit. Your Communications Director quit. Your son-in-law lost his security clearance. You started a trade war because you were grumpy. Your campaign aide got subpoenaed, but not before he could go insane on national television. And, oh yeah, you're being sued by the porn star you had an affair with because you were too dumb to sign the NDA you had made to cover it all up!
This calls for a cold drink! SLLUURP!
No chaos...
Just great energy!
TRU
Sod
"Tastes like Bankrupt

Mar 9, 2018

Mar 13, 2018

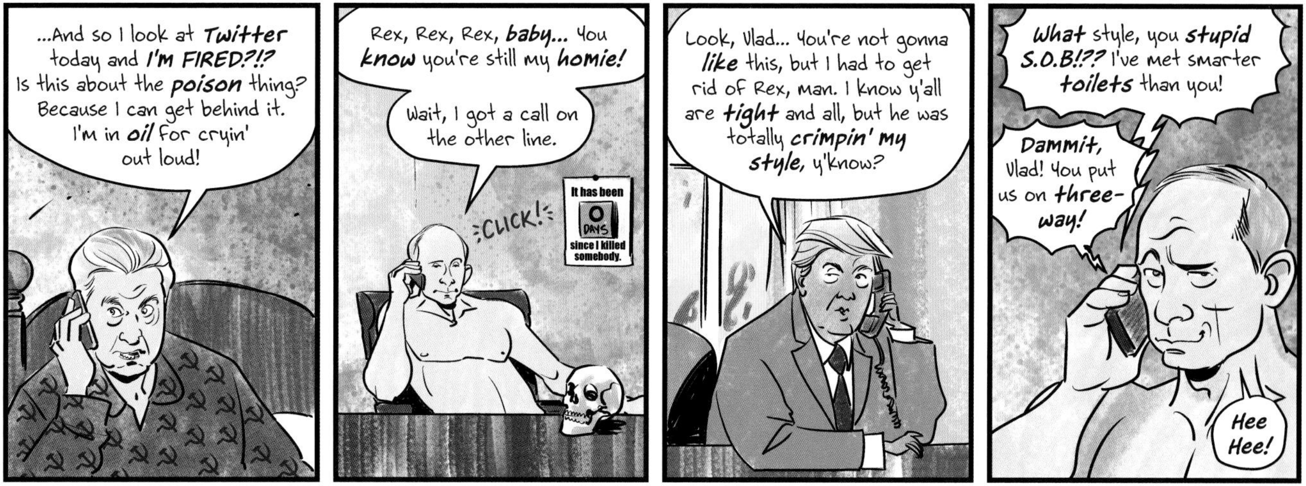
...And so I look at Twitter today and I'M FIRED?!? Is this about the poison thing? Because I can get behind it. I'm in oil for cryin' out loud!
Rex, Rex, Rex, baby... You know you're still my homie!
Wait, I got a call on the other line.
CLICK!
It has been 0 DAYS since I killed somebody.
Look, Vlad... You're not gonna like this, but I had to get rid of Rex, man. I know y'all are tight and all, but he was totally crimpin' my style, y'know?
What style, you stupid S.O.B!?? I've met smarter toilets than you!
Dammit, Vlad! You put us on three-way!
Hee Hee!

Mar 15, 2018

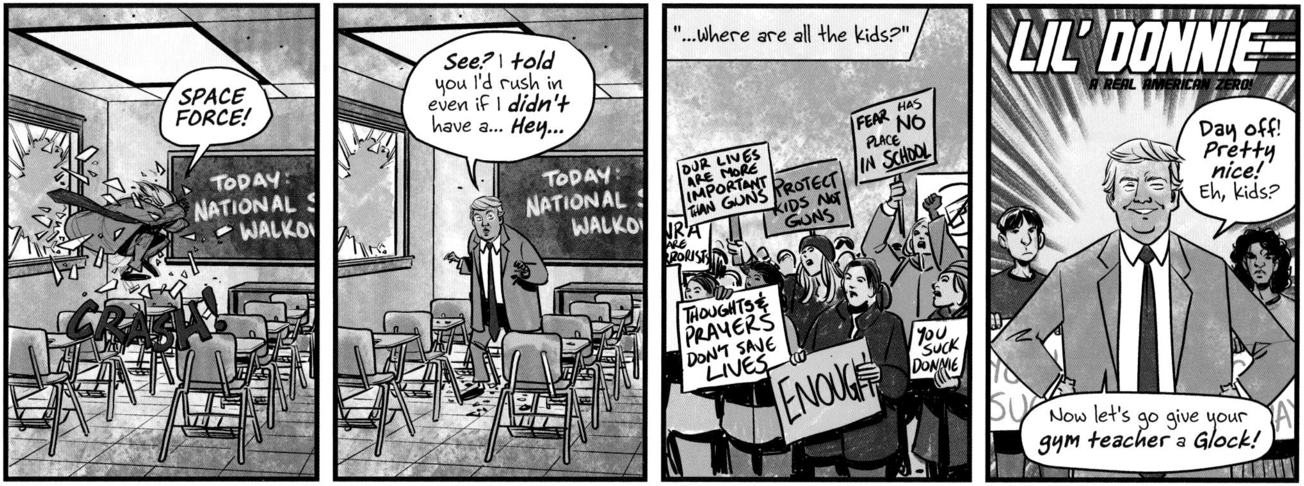
SPACE FORCE!
CRASH!
See? I told you I'd rush in even if I didn't have a... Hey...
"...Where are all the kids?"
OUR LIVES ARE MORE IMPORTANT THAN GUNS
PROTECT KIDS NOT GUNS
FEAR HAS NO PLACE IN SCHOOL
THOUGHTS & PRAYERS DON'T SAVE LIVES
ENOUGH
YOU SUCK DONNIE
LIL' DONNIE
A REAL AMERICAN ZERO!
Day off! Pretty nice! Eh, kids?
Now let's go give your gym teacher a Glock!

Mar 21, 2018

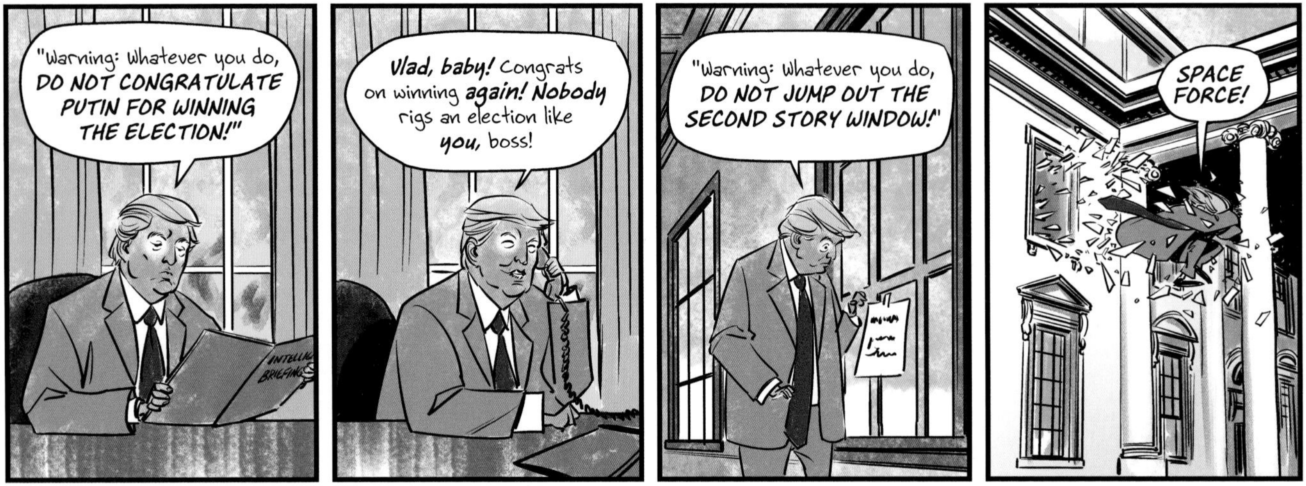
"Warning: Whatever you do, DO NOT CONGRATULATE PUTIN FOR WINNING THE ELECTION!"
Vlad, baby! Congrats on winning again! Nobody rigs an election like you, boss!
"Warning: Whatever you do, DO NOT JUMP OUT THE SECOND STORY WINDOW!"
SPACE FORCE!

Mar 22, 2018

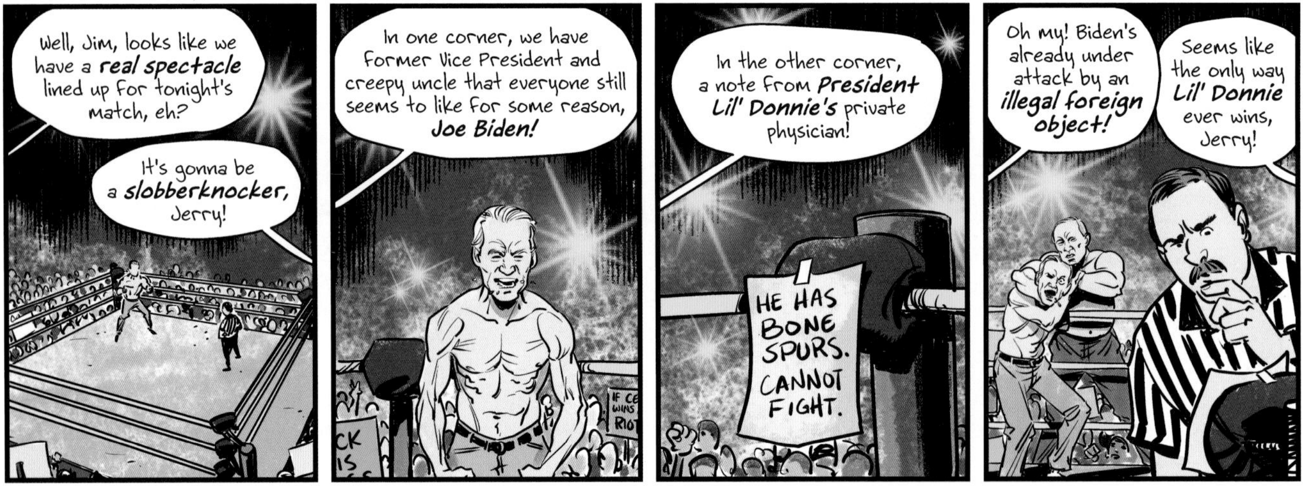
Well, Jim, looks like we have a real spectacle lined up for tonight's match, eh?
It's gonna be a slobberknocker, Jerry!
In one corner, we have former Vice President and creepy uncle that everyone still seems to like for some reason, Joe Biden!
In the other corner, a note from President Lil' Donnie's private physician!
HE HAS BONE SPURS. CANNOT FIGHT.
Oh my! Biden's already under attack by an illegal foreign object!
Seems like the only way Lil' Donnie ever wins, Jerry!

Mar 26, 2018

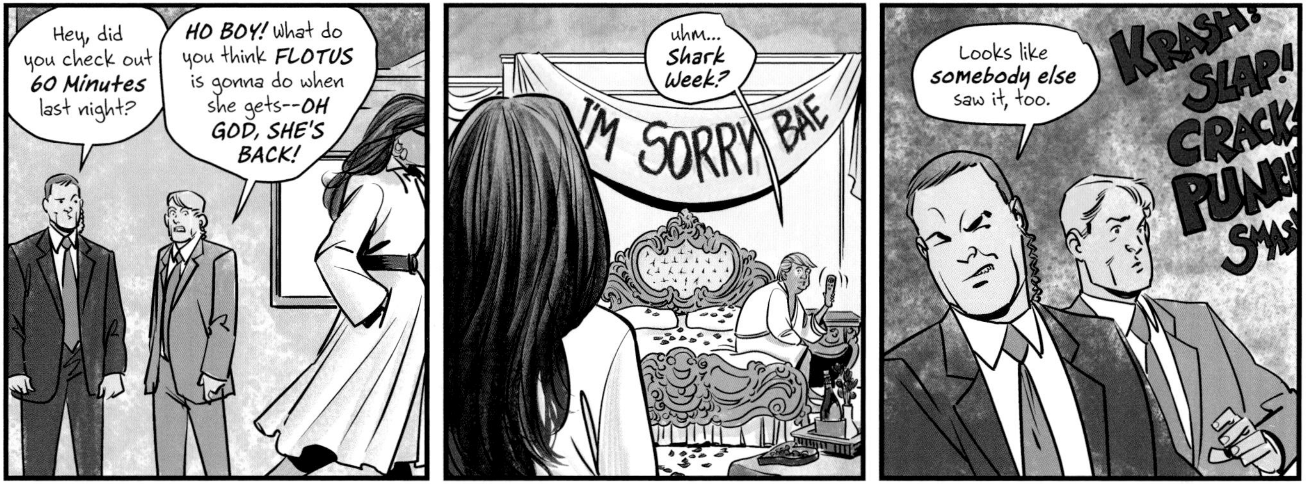
Hey, did you check out **60 Minutes** last night?
HO BOY! What do you think **FLOTUS** is gonna do when she gets--**OH GOD, SHE'S BACK!**
I'M SORRY BAE
uhm... **Shark Week?**
Looks like **somebody else** saw it, too.
KRASH!
SLAP!

Mar 29, 2018

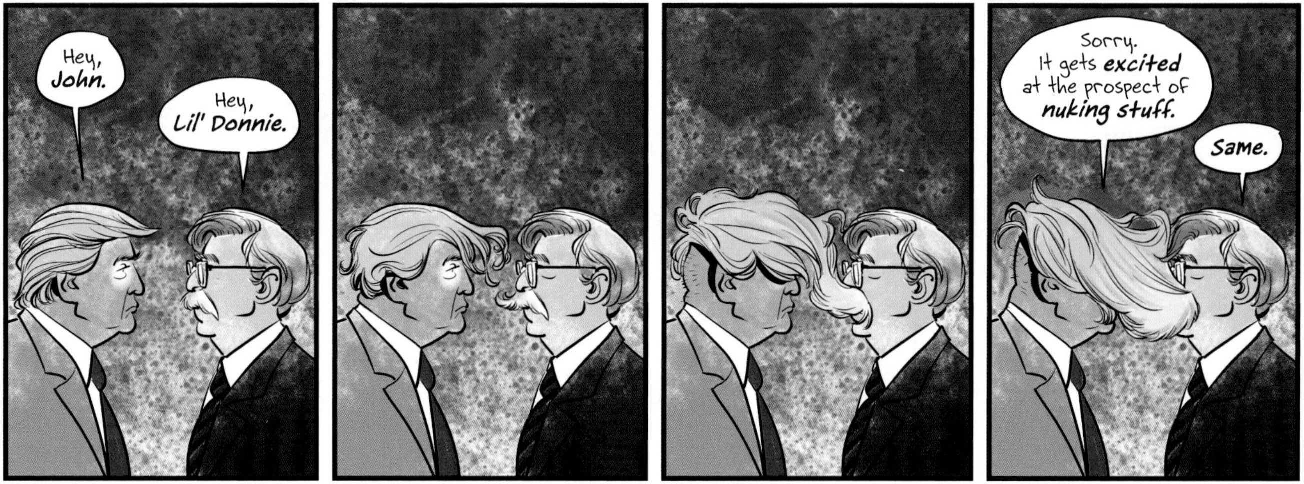
Hey, **John.**
Hey, **Lil' Donnie.**
Sorry. It gets **excited** at the prospect of **nuking stuff.**
Same.

Apr 2, 2018

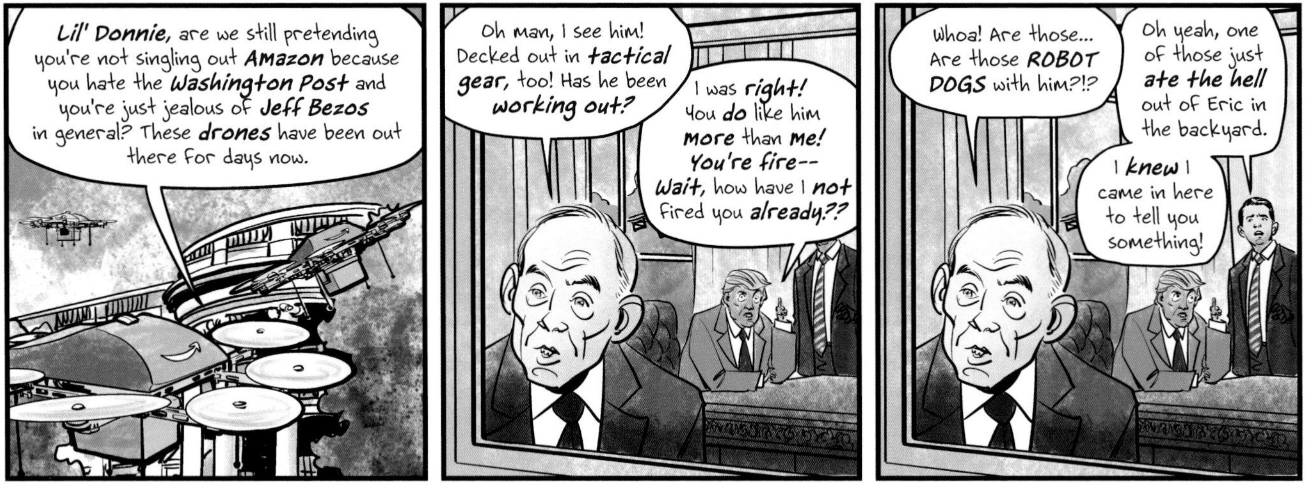

Lil' Donnie, are we still pretending you're not singling out Amazon because you hate the Washington Post and you're just jealous of Jeff Bezos in general? These drones have been out there for days now.
Oh man, I see him! Decked out in tactical gear, too! Has he been working out?
I was right! You do like him more than me! You're fire-- Wait, how have I not fired you already??
Whoa! Are those... Are those ROBOT DOGS with him?!?
Oh yeah, one of those just ate the hell out of Eric in the backyard.
I knew I came in here to tell you something!

Apr 10, 2018

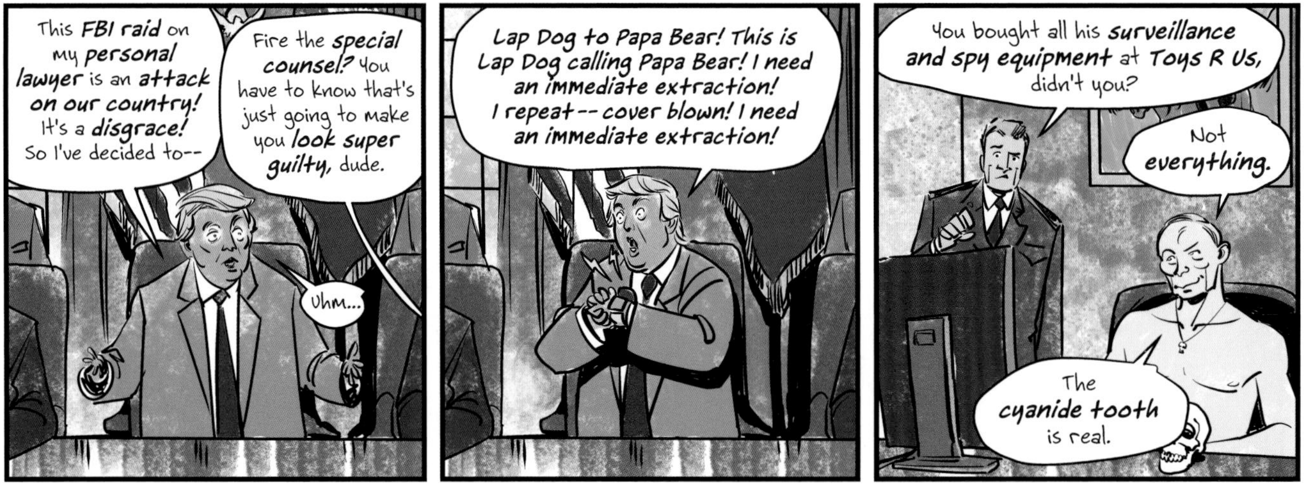

This FBI raid on my personal lawyer is an attack on our country! It's a disgrace! So I've decided to--
Fire the special counsel? You have to know that's just going to make you look super guilty, dude.
Uhm...
Lap Dog to Papa Bear! This is Lap Dog calling Papa Bear! I need an immediate extraction! I repeat -- cover blown! I need an immediate extraction!
You bought all his surveillance and spy equipment at Toys R Us, didn't you?
Not everything.
The cyanide tooth is real.

Lil' Donnie

by Mike Norton

Apr 13, 2018

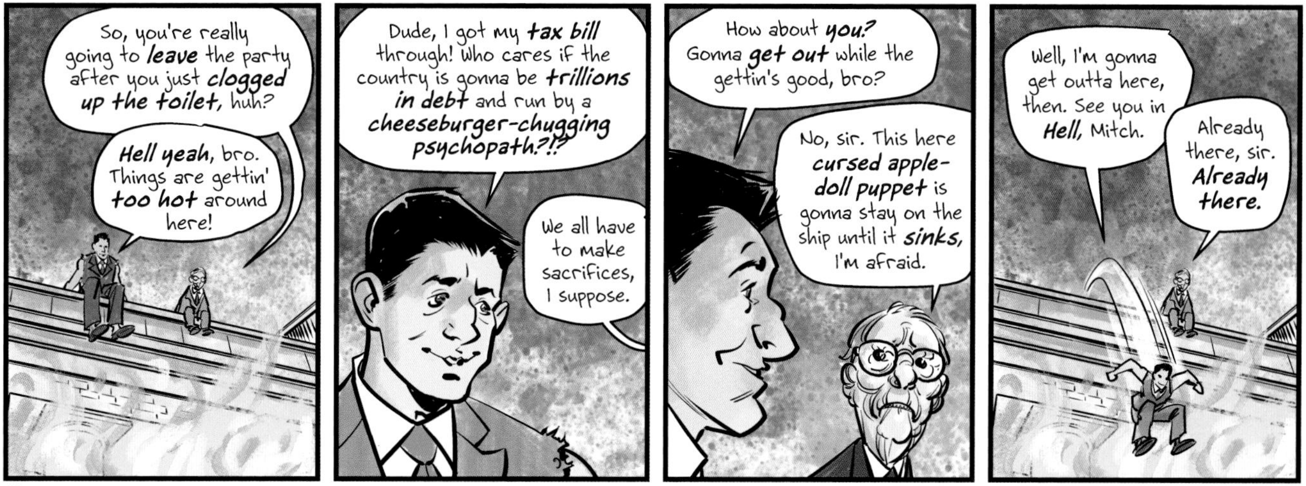
So, you're really going to leave the party after you just clogged up the toilet, huh?
Hell yeah, bro. Things are gettin' too hot around here!
Dude, I got my tax bill through! Who cares if the country is gonna be trillions in debt and run by a cheeseburger-chugging psychopath?!?
We all have to make sacrifices, I suppose.
How about you? Gonna get out while the gettin's good, bro?
No, sir. This here cursed apple-doll puppet is gonna stay on the ship until it sinks, I'm afraid.
Well, I'm gonna get outta here, then. See you in Hell, Mitch.
Already there, sir. Already there.

lildonniecomic.com

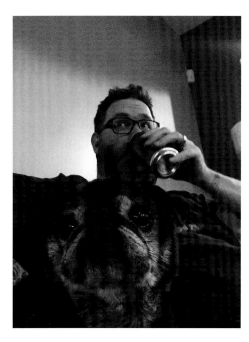

MIKE NORTON is the creator of the Harvey and Eisner Award-winning webcomic, *Battlepug* and the co-creator and artist of *Revival*. [redacted]. He has worked for Marvel, [redacted], DC, Dark Horse and just about everybody else. He's currently drawing a webcomic called LIL' DONNIE about the worst president in US history. [redacted]. He lives in Chicago with his wife, two pugs, and a fridge full of beer.

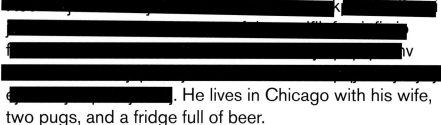

OTHER BOOKS BY MIKE NORTON

BATTLEPUG VOLUME 1: BLOOD AND DROOL
w/ Allen Passalaqua and crank! | ISBN 978-1-59582-9726

BATTLEPUG VOLUME 2: THIS SAVAGE BONE
w/ Allen Passalaqua and crank! | ISBN 978-1-61655-2015

BATTLEPUG VOLUME 3: SIT. STAY. DIE!
w/ Allen Passalaqua and crank! | ISBN 978-1-61655-5948

BATTLEPUG VOLUME 4: THE DEVIL'S BISCUIT
w/ Allen Passalaqua and crank! | ISBN 978-1-61655-8642

BATTLEPUG VOLUME 5: THE PAWS OF WAR
w/ Allen Passalaqua and crank! | ISBN 978-1-50670-1141

REVIVAL VOLUME 1: YOU'RE AMONG FRIENDS
w/ Tim Seeley, Mark Englert and crank! | ISBN 978-1-60706-6590

REVIVAL VOLUME 2: LIVE LIKE YOU MEAN IT
w/ Tim Seeley, Mark Englert and crank! | ISBN 978-1-60706-7542

REVIVAL VOLUME 3: A FARAWAY PLACE
w/ Tim Seeley, Mark Englert and crank! | ISBN 978-1-60706-8600

REVIVAL VOLUME 4: ESCAPE TO WISCONSIN
w/ Tim Seeley, Mark Englert and crank! | ISBN 978-1-63215-0127

REVIVAL VOLUME 5: GATHERING OF WATERS
w/ Tim Seeley, Mark Englert and crank! | ISBN 978-1-63215-3791

REVIVAL VOLUME 6: THY LOYAL SONS & DAUGHTERS
w/ Tim Seeley, Mark Englert and crank! | ISBN 978-1-63215-4729

REVIVAL VOLUME 7: FORWARD
w/ Tim Seeley, Mark Englert and crank! | ISBN 978-1-63215-9014

REVIVAL VOLUME 8: STAY JUST A LITTLE BIT LONGER
w/ Tim Seeley, Mark Englert and crank! | ISBN 978-1-5343-0056-9

THE ANSWER!
w/ Dennis Hopeless, Mark Englert, and crank! | ISBN 978-1-61655-197-1

MIKE NORTON'S THE CURSE
ISBN 978-1-934964-88-0

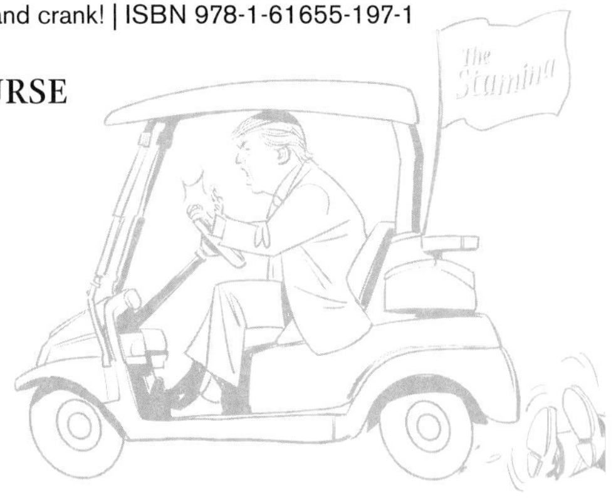

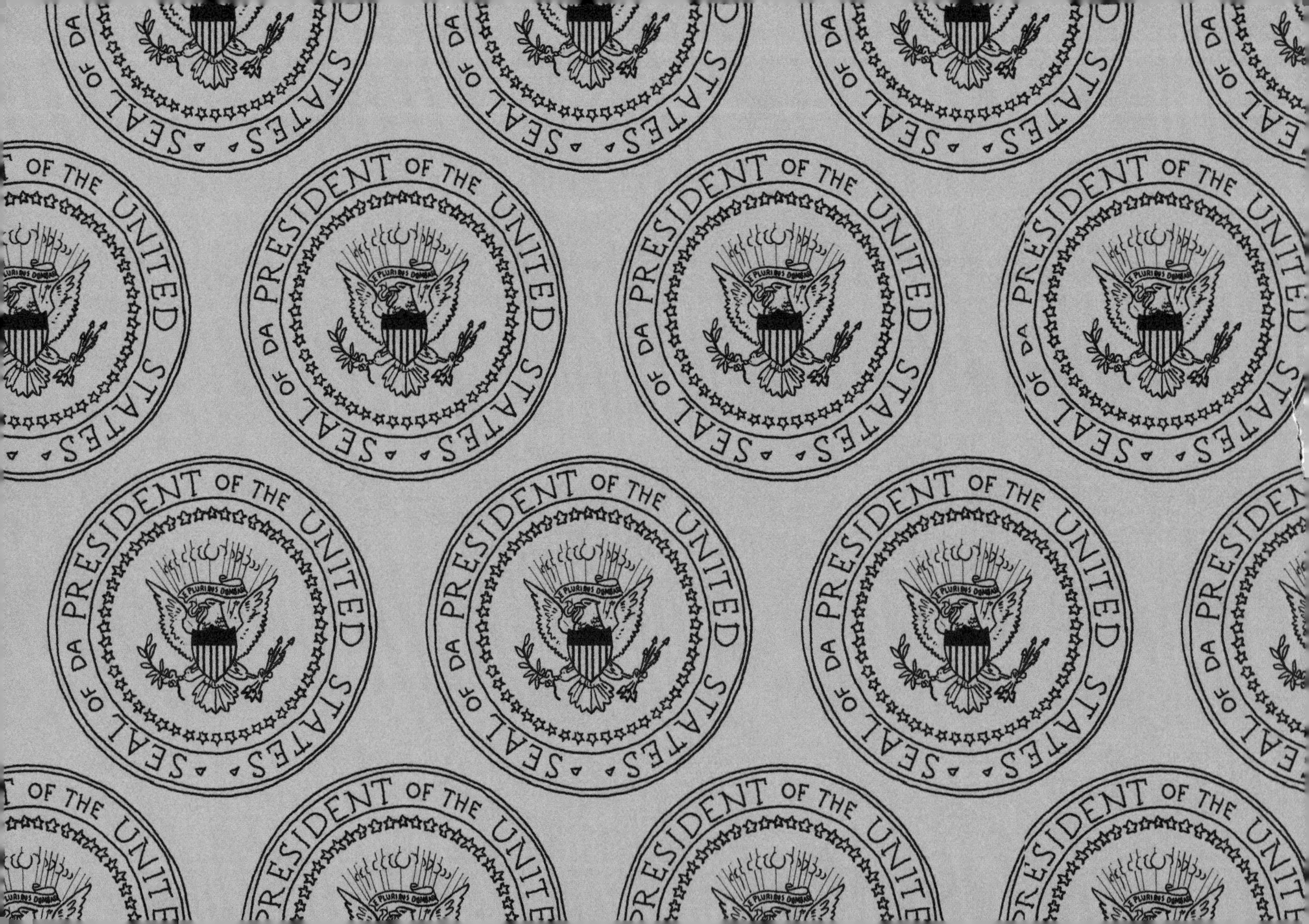
SEAL OF DA PRESIDENT OF THE UNITED STATES